for Rachel, Harper, and Jesse

Creativity for Sale

Radim Malinic

First published in the United Kingdom in 2023 by Brand Nu, brandnubooks.co.uk

**Creativity For Sale** - How to *start* and grow a life-changing *creative* career and business

Copyright ©2023 Radim Malinic

1

The right of Radim Malinic to be identified as author of this work has been asserted by him in accordance with the Copyright, Design and Patent Act 1988.

Written by Radim Malinic

Editor Ameesha Green

Cover illustration Timo Kuilder

Illustrator Emily Melling

Proofreader  Gemma Rowlands

Proofreader  Shelby Jones

Creative direction + design Radim Malinic

British Library Cataloguing-in-Publication Data A catalogue record for this book is available from the British Library

All rights reserved. No part of this publication may be reproduced or transmitted in any form or by any means, electronic or mechanical, including photocopy, recording or any other information storage and retrieval system, without prior permission in writing from the publisher.

Brand Nu is a registered trademark of Brand Nu Limited.

**Made in London, England**

Printed by Park Communications on FSC® certified paper. Park works to the EMAS standard and its Environmental Management System is certified to ISO 14001.

This publication has been manufactured using 100% offshore wind electricity sourced from UK wind.

100% of the inks used are vegetable oil based, 95% of press chemicals are recycled for further use and, on average 99% of any waste associated with this production will be recycled and the remaining 1% used to generate energy.

This book is printed on Edixion Offset paper made of material from well-managed, FSC®-certified forests and other controlled sources.

This is a certified climate neutral print product for which carbon emissions have been calculated and offset by supporting recognised carbon offset projects. The carbon offset projects are audited and certified according to international standards and demonstrably reduce emissions.

The climate neutral label includes a unique ID number specific to this product which can be tracked at climatepartner.com, giving details of the carbon offsetting process including information on the emissions volume and the carbon offset project being supported.

To find out more about this publication or the author, visit **radimmalinic.co.uk** or **brandnubooks.co.uk**

ISBN 978-0-9935400-4-2 [paperback]

Also available as ebook and audiobook

4

Creativity for Sale

How to *start* and grow a
life-changing *creative* career
and **business**

Radim Malinic

Brand Nu®

Creativity for Sale

Radim Malinic

## Contents

09. *Introduction*
18. Creativity for Sale
40. Power of One
72. Define  96. Build
118. Amplify  144. Money
170. Clients
192. Tools
206. Grow
228. *Bonus Content*

Creativity for Sale

## Creativity can change your life

It was a bright, sunny February morning with temperatures easily stretching over 30°C. The air was so humid that it felt like I was walking through a wall of hot air. An endless stream of motorbikes were whizzing up and down the road as I walked. When my bare feet touched the blistering hot, black sand beach, it was a mere hour after 17 hours in the skies (most of it spent awake and giddy about the prospect of my trip). There I was, finally — on Canggu Beach in Bali — all kitted out in my brand-new surf gear, heading out into the shimmering, turquoise waters. The waves looked incredible, and I felt like a kid on Christmas morning about to take my new toy for a spin. I felt unstoppable. As it turned out, I wasn't.

Within moments, the giant Indonesian ocean waves knocked me into a total wipeout. I was submerged under the water, under my board, tumbling and turning below the surf in a desperate bid to get back to shore. It was a tragicomic performance, and just minutes after getting my breath back on the glistening sand, I wondered how on earth I had thought I could pull off this kind of stunt.

Admittedly, I knew it didn't look easy before I even put a foot on that surfboard, but I let my misplaced confidence and enthusiasm get the better of me. It was a sobering reminder that I needed a lot more practice if I were to get even close to surfing those big waves properly. Not that I really wanted to admit it at the time, but I'd skipped the crucial foundational steps that would have helped me ride the waves instead of wiping out. The basic prior experience and knowledge that I was equipped with wasn't anywhere near enough for the 7-foot-tall fast-rolling swells.

Perhaps predictably, that wasn't the only time in my life where action preceded thought. I've always had a tendency to jump headfirst into situations, be it bands, DJing, music journalism, or product lines. I even joined an ice hockey team before I could skate properly... In fact, my life motto seems to have been: "Why make a plan when you can work it all out later?"

Now, you might be wondering what surfing in Bali has to do with creativity or business. Well, the way I approached starting a creative business is a lot like the way I approached surfing: TLDR. I wasn't interested in the logistics of a new endeavour, nor keen on dwelling on the details of what was to come. *If other people can do it*, I often reasoned, *then why couldn't I?* This wasn't necessarily the right way of approaching either task, but it was the way I chose. It was the creative's way. With my surfing story, it was the idiot's way.

Somewhere on that often-uncomfortable journey, I realised that creativity can change your life. It certainly changed my life, though not without learning a lot of lessons along the way, most of them the hard way. Sure, it rarely worked out perfectly for me the first time – nor the second, if we're being honest – but I always persevered with my new endeavour, and eventually I started paddling in the right direction, spotting the right waves, and taking that leap up onto my board.

I also found a way to appreciate that creativity is an ongoing journey of discovery, where you're always meeting new and incredible people, learning varied and valuable skills, and picking up useful and interesting knowledge. In the creative industries, everyone's experiences are different; it is a melting pot of different backgrounds, skills, knowledge, and life encounters, and that's what makes it wonderful.

So here's the disclaimer: this book is written from my own personal experiences, observations, and knowledge. The information and advice is gathered from my own real-life experience of running a small creative business and navigating the choppy waters of the last economic crash, the Covid-19 pandemic, and the cost of living crisis. It's based on what I've seen, heard, and learned, and I fully acknowledge that what works for one person might not always or ever work for the next. But I would also argue that more often than not, there are certain things that most of us can agree on, and this book toes the line between the two.

It doesn't matter if you don't know what or where you want to be right now. The important thing, as cliched as it may sound,

Creativity for Sale

is that you have the courage to start something. I'm not saying that you should do what I did and run head-first into those epic Bali waves without any idea of how to surf, but I am saying that you can never meticulously plan for every twist and turn of the journey ahead, nor will every part of it always be enjoyable.

I can promise you that some of it will definitely suck; sometimes you will miss the wave, sometimes you will wipe out, and other times, your board will hit you on the head as you struggle to see which way is up. But in those moments, try to laugh at yourself and laugh at the situation. You're only one wave away from getting right.

Always strive to have fun in what you do, to stay curious, and to learn from your inevitable mistakes. That's what creativity is all about, whether it is creativity in your personal life, like learning a new hobby, or creativity for sale, in your business life.

If you keep these simple points in mind, creativity will change your life, just like it changed mine.

## Preface

As you've picked up (or clicked on) a book called *Creativity for Sale*, I would hope that you're curious about exploring your creativity and potentially building a business around your skills, talents, and ideas. Maybe you're considering starting that journey and don't know which direction to head in. Maybe you're already on that journey and are looking for guidance to move forward. Maybe you've been on that journey for a while and feel like you've lost your way. This book will help you get moving.

One of the overarching themes of this book is guiding you along the path to sustainable and robust creative business. This means it outlines the importance of spending time building the foundations of that business: that bedrock could mean the difference between surviving shaky economic climates or crumbling. Strong business foundations mean that the fun bit — the creative part of a creative business — can truly flourish.

You will also see the importance of forging creative partnerships, understand how to make your clients feel that they are part of a collaborative team, and realise how those relationships will underpin your long-term success. Importantly, you will learn how to start planting the seeds of the meaningful connections that will lead to the right opportunities and help work find you. It's all about building a brand based around you and your unique creative outlook.

So, what makes this book different from the plethora of other books about starting a creative business? First off, this book was designed to be universal and apply to whichever facet of the creative industries is relevant to you — whether you're working directly with small independent clients, collaborating with big name brands, or freelancing for established creative teams; whether you craft visual identities, write brand copy, or pen bespoke jingles. This book is for any solo-creative who sees themselves as being (now or in the future) more than a freelancer — someone who is running their own small creative business. It isn't a prescriptive guide where you should do absolutely everything I say, but it is first-hand guidance you can pick and choose from on your journey.

While no one can ever be truly prepared for every challenge or situation (I've said it before and I'll say it again), this book will arm you with the skills needed to navigate the intricacies of this way of working, and the daily problem-solving that will be required of you. It will also help you put the right frameworks in place to have a prosperous and above all fun creative career.

So, are you ready to catch your wave?

## Creativity for Sale
From page 18

This first chapter will start you on the road to building your own creative business. You'll discover the 'power of one' and understand how 'creativity for sale' can change your life. You'll see the importance of creative bravery, get a dose of realism, and see how creativity becomes a business. Then you'll be ready to take your first steps in the world of business.

## Power of One
From page 40

In the next chapter, we'll dive deeper into 'the power of one'. You'll learn that no one is ever ready and there are no overnight successes, but you'll locate your parachute and pack what you need for the journey ahead to motivate you and keep you going. You'll learn how to deal with negativity, start leaning into being yourself, and begin living and breathing what you do.

## Define
From page 72

Now it's time to start getting more defined, so here you'll get more detailed guidelines to define you and your unique offering. With plenty of prompts and questions to help you piece together your unique business strategy (or manifesto), you'll start to define your current and future efforts. You'll start to define your expectations, what your version of success looks like, and your goals.

Creativity for Sale

## Build

Then we'll start building your personal brand, covering the essentials of getting seen and becoming known — from your visual strategy and naming your business to choosing your domain, curating your portfolio, and driving and owning your traffic. We'll also consider social media, emails, branded stationery, and even your personal wardrobe.

## Amplify

Amplify offers a series of suggestions to find and make meaningful connections with your future clients and collaborators — and make sure these 'targets' are aware that your business exists. There's nothing more essential than long-term value clients who will keep you happy, busy, and financially afloat. We'll cover the importance of messaging, websites, and how to talk the talk.

## Money

Throughout your career, it might feel as though you spend as much time chasing invoices, sending estimates, and navigating budget negotiations with clients. But it doesn't have to be like that, and this chapter shares secrets that help you deal with all things financial like setting your prices, quoting, and billing for projects when the time comes.

## Clients
From page 170

Working with and for others can open up a lot of new horizons, but it can also be a challenge. That's why this chapter is all about getting enquiries, turning them into live projects, dealing with clients, managing emotions, and delivering work that's on time, on budget, and beyond expectations. That way, you'll keep your clients happy and keep your business going.

## Tools
From page 192

The day-to-day realities of running a business — like admin tasks, promotional activities, scheduling meetings, replying to emails, managing projects, and seeking feedback — can feel endless. That's why this section offers a range of useful business and creative tools that are available to help, so you can automate as much of the behind-the-scenes stuff as possible.

## Grow
See page 206

Every day in your business might be different to the last, and the only thing that's constant in life is change. For that reason, this final chapter looks at how to keep going, how to spin plates, and how to grow from your mistakes. You'll also see the importance of making marginal gains, tracking your progress, growing your team, and choosing your problems. It's time to grow!

Creativity for Sale

pages

18 — 39

Chapter - no.1

# Creativity for Sale

Creativity for Sale

**Chapter - no.1**

23. The road ahead
25. *Creativity for sale*
26. Creative bravery
28. *This is business*
29. Taking the first few steps
31. *How selling creativity becomes a business*
36. The 'do what you love' myth

Creativity for Sale

22

Creativity for Sale

## The road ahead

The central premise of this book is that it's possible (in fact, more than possible) to build your career and business around your unique set of skills, talents, and creative ideas, that is, your very own brand of creativity. This is because no one else's approach will be quite the same as yours.

However, starting *your* own creative business means taking control of your life and your career by harnessing your creativity, and this will likely mean starting off small — and on your own. Running any kind of business, creative or not, involves you personally scaling a metaphorical mountain again and again, where the peak might seem further away every time you reach a brow. And there's no denying that there will be a lot of bumps and rocks on the path ahead. It might be hard at times, but it should never be dull (and if it feels that way, then you can always take a different path and use your energy in a way that inspires you and makes you want to get up in the morning).

There will be lows, and they will hurt. There will also be magical highs, and they will feel great. And in the end, it'll be so worth it. Around the world, millions of people are finally pursuing their dreams, and plenty of them are wishing they'd started doing it sooner. Despite the challenges, they are celebrating what they have personally achieved.

And because you're setting off on this path alone most of the time, you can and should be your own personal cheerleader, coach, mentor, or even therapist. At times, it might feel as though the odds are stacked against you, and that it's almost impossible to achieve what you truly want, but your life can be as creative as you allow it to be. And you're not on your own as from here on in, you can consider me to be your biggest cheerleader and number one fan. If I managed to do it, you can ace it too.

You might feel small right now, but a small creative business is just a microscopic fraction of the overall industry, and a smaller fraction of what makes up the nation's economy. The word 'small' doesn't mean that its impact should be underestimated. On the contrary, design-led creative businesses lead the charge of innovation, crafting the experiences and products that drive the future forward. Every single one of them began the same way you're starting your business today. You just never know what lies ahead, and that's the most exciting part.

Whatever size your business will become, you should feel empowered to stand tall and proud that you have a unique voice amongst the countless others out there. So, pursue your mission with energy and conviction — and remember that everyone starts small.

## Creativity for sale

'Creativity' and 'business' are two concepts that seem to go hand in hand while also contradicting one another, like a couple who get on like a house on fire but also have blazing arguments. The upshot of this is that the most gifted artist can also be the lousiest businessperson, and vice versa. To succeed on this path, knowing how to get paid for your creativity is vital, and there's no excuse for pleading ignorance (at least after you've finished this book).

There's also no need to park your creative dream and delve into endless books about business and economics before you get started. Following your heart and building your dream business should be your sole focus, and you will learn a lot as you go (though perhaps not as dramatically as I did with surfing). This book will help you establish, or reconsider, the fundamentals of what you need to establish a smooth commercial operation.

The only things you need to get started are your 'fuel' and 'feel', your magic formula, and the superpower you will turn into a creative business. The good news is you already have these essential ingredients — and this book will help you identify them. Then, the next step is to put them in the spotlight for the world to see.

Your 'magic formula' isn't something short-term or on-trend; it's the thing that makes you light up because you are doing what feels right for your soul; it comes naturally and no one else can replicate it (don't worry, the 'Define' chapter includes various exercises to help you identify it). It is not inspired by what you are currently seeing or hearing, or a current trend you find particularly exciting and that seems to offer a tantalising shortcut to guarantee early interest and results. It's right inside your soul.

This magic formula is one of the essential parts of your 'Creativity for Sale' equation; it is the beginning of your personal brand of creativity. And these pages are here to guide you towards the right pathway to establish your own creative expression unique to you — something I call 'the power of one'.

## Creative bravery

Some of us may not realise this, but we're all born with the gift of creativity. Even as a baby, we display many creative tendencies in the decisions we make, in our curiosity, in the way we experience the world sensorially, and in how we build and make things, however rudimentary these things might be.

Equipped with crayons, poster paints, and/or glue sticks, children are often artistic powerhouses, churning out work far faster than their works of art can feasibly be displayed on the already growing art collection stuck on the fridge in every family kitchen. The reason for this intense work rate is because children don't worry about 'strategy'; they don't bother with mood boards, sketches, planning, and swatches, and they don't worry about feedback from their peers, contemporaries, or clients. They don't worry about the outcome. They are entirely focused on the act of making, creating, and exploring, and so their work is raw, unfiltered, and uncensored. They get lost in the process and stay there for a while.

Sadly, this devil-may-care attitude to creativity is often bashed out of us; sometimes at school with a flippant, unkind word from an art teacher; sometimes through parents more concerned about their offspring getting a 'proper job' than exercising their creative muscle; and often through an education system that underfunds and underappreciates the value of expression and creative flair. In society's way of thinking, creativity isn't what we should strive for in a career. It takes on different forms and doesn't always show us our career path ahead.

We're also often our own worst enemies here, because as we get older, we become more concerned about what others think of us and we fret so much about making things 'perfect' that we actually stifle our creativity into inertia. Indeed, one of the most valuable things to remember in a creative career (or hobbyist art-making) is that nothing will ever be perfect, and it doesn't need to be perfect for you to put it out there into the world.

What this means is if you're thinking of, or are in the process of, starting a creative business of one, then whether you feel 'creatively talented' or 'creatively strong enough' right now should not be a barrier. It's okay not to be perfect and it's okay to offer yourself and your creative services to the world anyway. You need to start somewhere and you might as well start now.

I understand that looking at the possibility of a creative career can feel extremely daunting, but the reality is that we can't do it all, we can't make it all, and we can't be perfect. It's normal to have concerns though, and you may be thinking: *Why bother? Everyone is more talented than me.* Well, they aren't necessarily more talented, but they are likely to be a bit further ahead on their journey than you, and that's fine. Nobody is born as a fully formed concert pianist, script writer, or coding guru. In the classic nature vs. nurture debate, even if we believe that some people are pre-naturally talented, we can all safely agree that they hone their skills through hours and hours of practice and learning.

Either way, simply thinking and believing *I'm going to do this* is the first step on your creative career, and the one that will take you where you want to go. It's time to take that first step.

## This is business

For some creatives, the problem is they think their sensibilities can't easily mix with business. They believe that their work is all about their art, and the grind of the yearly tax return and other admin activities feel so unfair.

I'm going to be brutal: there's an option for such people, and it's called employment. It often comes with a smaller salary and less control or autonomy, but other people take care of the admin stuff. Ultimately, though, your creativity is in the hands of others.

By contrast, accepting the necessity of a business mindset is the first step towards longevity and potential success. It opens doors — many of them, and for a very long time. All of the extra admin doesn't show up right away, but it sure creeps up over time.

Through this book, you'll learn how to get help with the workload, automate the basic and time-consuming simple tasks, and build a team so you can do the things that motivate you to get up in the morning. But you have to accept that at least a certain amount of admin is part of being a small business owner, especially until you can pay someone to take it all off your hands.

In the long term, being at the helm of your business will pay off in that you get to choose where you want to be and how you want to get there. So, in the meantime, learn how to make it work. Adapt it for excellence. And suck up a little bit of admin.

## Taking the first few steps

An idea, skill, or talent is usually transformed into a business thanks to desire and passion, and it's exceptionally rare that a creative business starts with a business plan, an official company name, and a tax registry. Why would you do all of that before you know what exactly you want to do?

While there are, of course, exceptions to the rule, the vast majority of creative businesses start trekking up the mountain range without knowing exactly where the journey is heading or how it will proceed. Today, wherever you are in the world, all you really need is a laptop and internet access, then you can register your business and be ready to trade within a day or two. Your creative product might not be past its first iteration, but the excitement and determination will get you to the foot of the mountain, maybe even armed with a shiny new domain name, website template, online store, and social media channels with no real plan.

Of course, as soon as you've made the invisible visible, certain issues will hurl towards you at the speed of light and the sound of thunder. Or, more accurately, it's often the whistle of tumbleweed. You're open for business and no one knows about it; that's the first big issue you have to solve. Then the business encounters its first client or customer, and at that point, your business plan (if you had one) becomes near obsolete. Everything can change as projection and potential meets reality.

I say this from experience. In my first failed attempt to become a 'freelance designer', I was smitten with the idea of the creative lifestyle, the possibility of making amazing work and meeting dream clients, and the vision of seeing my designs loud and proud up and down the country. Except, of course, it didn't happen quite the way I'd imagined.

Like many others, I started out with a laptop loaded with creative applications (some, perhaps, obtained through slightly questionable sources, ahem) and was duly subscribed to all the industry magazines possible. The 'thing' I wanted to do happened before it became a 'business thing'. In other words, the guitar before the gig (or the ability to play one). Words before language. It was the surfboard all over again.

In my passionate yet naïve quest to pursue a design career, I had failed to identify the many essential parts that would turn my super keen energy (the fuel) into an actual, moving business, like I had no idea how to build a regular clientele list, I had no creative philosophy beyond being a guy who was happy to design pretty much anything to pay the rent, and I had no coherent portfolio to show any potential clients. I was armed with a meagre business card, and aside from that, I had no clients and no idea. Although I managed to get a few semi-regular commissions and support myself to some extent, the whole episode, perhaps unsurprisingly, didn't last long. As soon as my overdraft and credit card were maxed out, I had to apply for a couple of in-house graphic design jobs to see me through, and thankfully I landed them.

Back in the employed world, I realised that my keenness wasn't enough to pay the bills, and I had a lot to learn before I would set up my small business, this time with a much better foundation for longevity. However, I also discovered that you learn a lot of lessons while you're on the journey, and you can't plan for every eventuality. There's no such thing, really, as being perfectly fully prepared, and no one is absolutely ready for the path ahead.

We're all lacing up our boots at the foot of the mountain, and we might need to change that pair based on the terrain we find ourselves facing, but if we don't take those first steps, we'll never get going.

## How selling creativity becomes a business

There are various ways that you can describe yourself as a creative business. Some prefer to be seen as a one-man-band; others prefer to act like a studio and imply a larger entity than the reality.

One thing to bear in mind is: the way we describe our business should be on par with what we actually are, and what we can deliver. In other words, there's no point pretending that you're a 20-person studio with a diversity of skills and project management if you're actually one individual juggling freelance work alongside a 9–5 job.

At some point, the client will discover the truth and things will fall apart.

There are a few different ways that you can label the business of selling creativity:

**Self-employed** - This means that you work for yourself as a business owner instead of being employed by somebody else. It means you are responsible for finding your own work, keeping records of your financial operations, and paying your taxes at the end of the financial year. In the creative industries, it's very rare that people describe themselves to customers or clients as 'self-employed', so you can think of this as a technical term to explain your business and tax status.

**Freelancer** - This is probably the most frequently used term for those starting out as their own creative entity, but it's also the most misunderstood. Ultimately, it's another way to describe being self-employed, but people often understand it to mean that the worker is flexible, readily available, and able to juggle multiple small projects and clients at any one time. For this reason, many people or companies seeking someone with a particular skill set temporarily use the prefix 'freelance' in internet searches e.g., 'looking for a freelancer designer/illustrator for a creative project'.
The problem is that when someone searches for a 'freelancer', they may have vastly different expectations about who will appear. I have met many prospective clients who searched for 'a freelance designer' (i.e., individual) then asked how big my studio (i.e., team) is. I have also found myself in a never-ending loop of enquiries either for something super basic or that required my operation to be much bigger than it really was.

It gets even more confusing because 'freelancers' can be broadly divided into two categories. The first work directly with clients, often multiple clients at once on various projects, in much the same way as a small studio might — doing the work and also marketing their own services to find clients. The second are hired by an agency or company to work, directly or indirectly, with clients, and often do very little to market themselves personally. While the former have to build a public-facing portfolio or 'creative brand' to attract clients, the latter often find work via recruitment agents or in-house planning teams.

A 'hired freelancer' (also known as a 'contractor') can be anything from a camera operator for a TV station to a runner on a production set, an SEO expert, web developer, or marketing executive. These freelancers don't usually deviate from their core skill set, and they often work in one place (such as in a creative agency or on location) for an extended period of time, much like a short-term employee working alongside full-time staff. Although hired freelancers operate in a similar way to employees, the label 'freelancer' can feel very liberating as it means they don't have to show up to the same old 9–5 job day in day out for years on end.

For the non-hired freelancers, they are often expected to be readily available for last-minute projects and willing to work longer hours than traditional employees. They tend to juggle many different assignments due to their unpredictable workstream, which can lead to oversubscribing and therefore overworking themselves. Despite this, being a pure freelancer is often a very appealing prospect compared to having a fixed salary and holiday allowance as it offers a level of flexibility and autonomy that is rare in any other type of work. It also creates opportunities to explore ideas and work on unusual projects that would be impossible in full-time employment.

**Contractor** - This is another technical term for self-employment, but it means specifically operating under a contract or agreement to provide services for the pre-agreed period of time, i.e., a hired freelancer (though in practice, most people and companies use the term 'freelancer' to cover both scenarios). A contractor is often booked for long stretches of time, working alongside full-time employees within a company during normal working hours. Unlike employees, however, the contractor doesn't get a holiday allowance or sick pay, and they are still responsible for their own tax, social security, and pension.

**Consultant -** The role of a consultant is less hands-on in terms of delivery or creative outcome than a freelancer. Their task is to evaluate the issues and provide an outline of how the solution can be reached. A consultant's involvement can range from a few days to ongoing support across longer periods of time.

**Small business** - This category is where you might see a local cake shop or 'a man with a van'. In UK government terms, they're likely to be officially classified as a 'micro business'. A small business in the UK means less than 250 employees and turning over less than £50 million a year, which you'd be forgiven for thinking isn't that small really! Despite the facts and figures of the official terminology, I believe that the best way to gain the confidence and presence to progress your creative journey is to adopt a 'small business mindset', as that's where the magic happens.

**Studio** - This is an operation of multiple people delivering projects within a specific sector, such as branding, animation, printmaking, etc. An established studio often has a number of different personnel looking after the clients' projects as well as the business operations. Despite this, 'studio' is also a popular term that individual freelancers use, even at the very beginning of their business life because the term suggests a more established outfit than 'freelancer'. As I mentioned earlier, there's a danger that clients might assume you have more capacity than you really do, so be sure not to upsell your capabilities unless you have a network of collaborators and skill-specific freelancers who can come on board to help with projects as needed.

**Agency** - This type of business goes beyond the scope of a studio, often employing hundreds of people with a myriad of skills beyond creative roles such as strategists, planners, and media buying experts. They usually service bigger clients than a studio does.

**The Rest** - Then there's the rest of the terms you might have come across… like 'solo creative' (means the same as freelancer), artist (a job type, not a way of working), musician (see previous), entrepreneur (small business owner who may or may not have a team), solopreneur (a small business owner who doesn't have a team), girl boss (a woman solo creative or small business owner), or hustler (don't get me started).

Ultimately, how you describe yourself is up to you, and some terms might feel more appealing and empowering to you personally, but it should be abundantly clear to your clients and your potential clients what you can actually deliver. If you try to mislead people with an incorrect label, you will likely end up over your head and unable to deliver, which might affect your ratings and reputation.

From experience, the longer you build your creative brand, the easier it becomes to let go of the label. New clients will be after what you do before they start wondering how you do it. Over time, you become known for your output and its trademark quality, and you will have a more fluid business setup. This often means that much bigger projects can land in your inbox due to your ability to deliver, rather than the label you describe it by. For now, pick the one that feels right and best sums up what you do.

## The 'do what you love' myth

Finally, it's time for a little dose of reality, because I really want this to be the right journey for you… In the world of work, the majority of jobs are simply about getting stuff done, not necessarily about loving what you do. Then there are, to the outside world, the exciting jobs like being a rock star or a performance artist, which we might love but unless we hit the big time, rarely seem to lead to financial stability. So, why is it that when it comes to the creative industries, we're sold the idea that "doing what you love" is almost guaranteed to go hand in hand with making enough money to jet away on nice holidays whenever we feel like it?

This notion fits into the cliché we've all heard no doubt numerous times: "If you do what you love, you'll never work a day in your life." Indeed, this phrase is banded around readily among business owners who get to choose their work. But the reality is that even for those who are utterly obsessed with and passionate about what they do, running a creative business isn't always (or even often!) a gentle stroll in the park. So, while this book only exists because I recommend that you take the leap to run your own creative service business, it would be naïve to think that being a business owner is all fun and games, even if you get to be more creative than most.

The truth is: running a creative business is still a lot of work. It might be a different kind of work, one that you (hopefully, if we get this right!) find fun and exciting, but it's also one that has to put the bread and butter on the table. On the surface, being creative might feel antithetical to being commercial, but every business, no matter what sector it operates in or what area of expertise it sits in, has to do the same thing when it comes to money, and that is: make some.

The problem is that when you sell creativity through the big 'machine' of commercial business operations, it can feel nigh-on impossible to work in a way that doesn't compromise your vision, creative freedom, and happiness. Running a business often means that the magical part where you actually get to be creative is limited to a few hours a day. Instead, you're pushing the business through the non-creative elements like admin, accounts, and client management (we'll look at these and how to ace them later on). And because of that, you might at some point find that you don't love what you do, or don't get to do what you love, anymore.

While there are many marvellous books on finding ways to enjoy your work as an employee, there are fewer that explore how to retain your love for what to do while also monetising it. That's why I'll be honest and open about what a creative career might look like for you, and lay out a strategy to widen that outlook even further so that your creative business is one you continue to love and enjoy.

# "If your ship doesn't come in, swim out to it!"

Jonathan Winters

Creativity for Sale

Pages
40 — 71

Chapter - no.2

# Power of One

## Chapter - no.2

**46.** *Power of you*
**47.** *No one is ever 'ready'*
**48.** *Locating your parachute*
**49.** *'The fuel' and 'the feel'*
**51.** *Your magic formula and your superpower*
**53.** *Freedom*
**54.** *There's no such thing as overnight success*
**55.** *The main investment: time*
**56.** *Battling negativity*
**57.** *Think and act like the person you want to become*

59. *Live and breathe what you want to do*
60. I do(n't) know what I'm doing
61. *Growth can happen in mysterious ways*
63. Self-taught or formal education?
64. *Being a shapeshifting creative*
66. Being the odd one out
67. *Being an alien*
69. The uneven starting line

Creativity for Sale

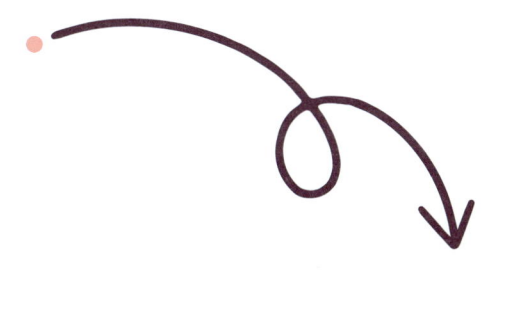

## Power of One

This and the following chapters will help you define, build, and amplify your own uniquely personal brand of creativity. By working through these stages, you can shape what people expect of you and your work, and how you're perceived.

Remember that crafting a personal brand isn't about trends or bandwagon-jumping; in fact, it's quite the opposite — it's about making sure the world knows who you are as a person by defining what you do as a creative professional, that is, the problems you can and will solve.

Consider these simple questions:

**What do you really want?**
**How much do you want it?**
**Who do you want to be?**
**How good do you want to be?**

## The power of you

Remember the power of one? Well, the power of one is actually the power of you.

It is your ability and willingness to create the future, to fix what you see is broken, and to invent what is missing. At this stage, it's impossible to know how big of an impact you might have in the future, but it should become clear very soon.

The key message of this book (yes, I am going to spell it out) is that you can build a life-changing and even world-changing career, business, and income from what you already have — from your collection of creative particles that make you unique. And contrary to what you might believe, you don't have to be a creative genius to get started.

As I explained in the previous chapter, you just need to get what you've got, take the first step, and then take another, and then a few more. If you keep looking up and moving forward, forging your own path, and ignoring the distractions that might derail you, then you will enjoy the journey you're on.

It's absolutely fine — in fact, it's even better — if you don't think you have what it takes to change the world, or even your world, right now. Many of us, myself included, didn't have a clue about what to do with our lives or careers at some point, but we set off in an unknown direction in search of our first destination regardless.

Once you empower yourself, you become the centre of gravity for your future.

## No one is ever 'ready'

If this is your starting line, how do you feel right now? Anxious, apprehensive, excited, relieved?

You might be telling yourself that you need to spend more time planning, thinking, and visualising. Maybe that extra work on your craft or your folio wouldn't go amiss, you tell yourself. The problem is, these might all be valid feelings. Or you might be making yourself believe you're not ready. As I said earlier and I'll no doubt say again, no one ever feels totally ready. And I'll be honest about this too: everyone feels scared at the beginning, even if they look super confident on the outside.

As long as you're willing to take the first step, you're on the way, and that's what really matters, not how confident you feel. And what then? Well, as humans, we often long for clarity about what's ahead of us, or at least that's what we make ourselves believe. But on the contrary, I would argue that when things become predictable, that's when it's time to wake up our senses — if everything we want to achieve in life is in front of us in plain sight, up for grabs without any effort required, we won't feel anywhere near the same sense of reward when we get them as the things we had to work harder for.

So, despite what we might believe, a certain amount of struggling and problem-solving is healthy on our journey; it's what makes it worth it.

## Locating your parachute

Of course, it would be remiss of me not to offer a word of warning, because 'no one is ever ready' does not mean you should hastily hand in your notice. Embarking on a self-driven creative journey might be the solution to escaping a job you hate, or perhaps going solo is simply the next step after education or a career change, or maybe it's about finally taking the plunge to make your dream happen. Whatever the reason, you should be at least somewhat prepared to make that leap.

I say this because every so often, a message lands in my inbox from someone who has just gone from employed to self-employed, and the question they always ask is, "What should I do next?" Every time I read such a message, I imagine the person standing at the door of a small aircraft, about to jump out without a parachute. Or in many cases, they've already leapt and are hurtling through the air while they're typing the email.

The reason why this happens is because some people become intoxicated by the prospect of running their own show, and so they take action from a place of excited naivety. I know this because once upon a time, I was that person, as I confessed earlier.

In my early 20s, I was first in the queue for that hypothetical parachute-less skydive. Even if I'd had a parachute, I still wouldn't have known how to use it. At the time, I would take any risks going as long as I didn't have to return to my crappy job. I desperately wanted to explore my creativity and was sure that a) there must be a way to do it, and b) there must be a way to get paid for it. So I jumped, and I had no idea where I was going, but I was going there fast, and with a massive smile on my face. Naturally, I crash-landed.

At that moment, it's impossible to press the rewind button and send the freshly self-employed person immediately back to the relative safety of an employed job. The lesson here is that if you're completely unprepared because you haven't thought it through, you can fall to the ground before you even start gliding. If you haven't spent time poring over the decisions that inform a big career leap, now is the time to do so. Each decision is a small piece of fabric, and together, they eventually form the parachute that ensures your safe landing.

## 'The fuel' and 'the feel'

Few of us can truly comprehend what a journey entails until we embark upon it. However, our combination of innocence and ignorance is what generates action, or more accurately, excitement and naivety. When you desire something so intensely that nothing and no one can deter you, then you disregard the harsh reality that lies ahead.

This is what I call 'the fuel': a necessarily blinkered view of where we want to go and how to get there without considering reality all that much. The fuel is any creative's trusty partner in crime. The fuel pushes you to make life-changing decisions; it's the fire-starter, the instigator, and the aggravator. It's the thing that gets you going on that journey in the first place. Just think about it; if you didn't have any fuel, your vehicle wouldn't even start.

That's not to say I'm making a case for pure chaos; after all, there wouldn't be much left of this book if that were the case. So, once you've used the fuel to start your engine, you'll need to work out where to steer. That's where fuel's counterpart, 'feel', comes in. The 'feel' is your natural decision-maker; it's connected to your soul and acts as your spiritual GPS, guiding you on which paths to take; where to direct and burn your fuel. And how do you find your 'feel'? Well, before the days of GPS, people navigated using the 'North Star', and many businesses still use this term today as the way they find direction.

Having a North Star is what turns a slacker into a powerhouse. It's also what stops people from panicking in a stressful business situation. But how do you find the North Star that gives you the direction, or 'feel', on your career journey? The answer is purpose i.e., the thing that makes you want to get out of bed in the morning and work the hours that you'd resent (or outright refuse) in your previous jobs. It is ultimately why you do what you do.

It's almost impossible to force people to do things they don't want to do, and no amount of persuading them will motivate them into action. We all need to be able to envision what we can do and how to do it ourselves.

As any parent knows, the best way to get a noisy child to quieten down isn't telling them to stop; it's giving them a role to play in the situation; it's giving them a purpose. And it gives your eardrums a break.

Purpose gives the journey a more defined shape, and a sense of direction. While most people have an inkling of how their creative work may have a positive impact on the bigger picture, they likely aren't aware of their exact purpose at the start of their career. For many people, their purpose only crystallises after many years of finding their feet.

Your purpose will come into sharper focus over time as your career develops and you understand your individual strengths and values. And while your purpose might change throughout your life and career, it will almost certainly have been there from the start; it could just take a while to spot it or be able to clearly articulate it. Purpose will become the 'feel' in how you approach your work and the way you make decisions about the future, as it provides clarity and direction in what you do.

Now, there are just two more items that you need to set off on that journey: your magic formula and your superpower. While your 'fuel' and 'feel' are your heart, your magic formula and superpower are your head.

## Your magic formula and your superpower

Your magic formula is the thing that makes you and your work unique. Everyone has a different set of talents, abilities, and passions, and this is their magic formula. Think of it a bit like how KFC have their secret blend of spices as, ultimately, this unique blend can form the basis of your very own personal brand.

Or in the context of our journey analogy, think of it as the unique combination of items that only you would pack in your travel luggage.

How to identify your **magic formula**:

— What is it that makes your work unique?
— What is your creative approach?
— What is your way of thinking?
— What are your passions?
— What activities make you lose track of time?
— What tasks come naturally to you?
— What lights you up?
— When do you feel most alive and fulfilled?

A magic formula then might be:

— Innovatively considering compositions
— Always being curious
— Working collaboratively
— Selecting colours and blending
— Having an eye for detail
— Illustrating things beautifully
— Valuing inclusion
— Making processes easier for people

Your superpower is, then, your ability to make your magic formula deliver time and time again; it is the strength needed to place your magic formula at the heart of your business and how it's run. Consider this to be your strongest strength, the thing that always gets you through. This superpower is the one thing that will keep your magic formula working time and time again.

How to recognise your **superpower**:

— Is there one word people often use to describe you?
— What one thing do others often praise or admire you for?
— What one thing has kept you going through tough times?
— If you could summarise your biggest strength in one word, what would it be?

Your superpower might be:

— Tenacity
— Patience
— Negotiation skills
— Resilience
— Flexibility/adaptability
— Financial acumen
— Mental strength

## Freedom

Just the thought of going solo or starting your own small creative business can make you feel transcendent and giddy with the excitement of finally being 'free'. Just imagine it: you call the shots, you set the alarm clock, and you can press the snooze button if you need to.

If you're making the leap from working 9–5 for someone else to working whatever hours you like for yourself, then some of the most tantalising parts of this new life might be waking up when you feel like it rather than when your office hours dictate, strolling downstairs to work instead of making the grim commute, and choosing your own projects instead of being handed them by somebody else.

As such, it can be tempting to think that you're going to quit your day job one week and be a fully-fledged successful freelancer the next. I've got news for you:

## There's no such thing as overnight success

When some bright new talent suddenly gets a tonne of press attention, seemingly out of nowhere, it can look like they've gone from zero to a hundred and are suddenly living the dream. To the outsider, their art looks brilliant and their 'creativity for sale' is perfect. As a result, they're landing all of the big commissions with the big-name dream brands, collaborating with the hottest artists, and appearing on the bill for every creative festival going.

However, the vast majority of the time, the reality is that they haven't been catapulted into 'creative industry darling' territory from nowhere. It might seem that way from the outside, but they've almost certainly been toiling away without most of their peers noticing — and certainly without the industry press paying any attention — for months, years, or even decades. In that time, they've been developing themselves and their skill set, and they have finally reached a point where both them and their work have something to say, and something that is considered 'worth talking about'.

Of course, there is always the exception to the rule, and a rare few make it to the top faster than most. However, while legions of new creatives are hungry for their time in the sun, they don't know how to handle the heat at that point, or appreciate how much it can burn them. In other words, once the initial flurry of publicity fades, the real test is maintaining that level of creativity into the future, and that's very challenging without a solid foundation in place.

This is why I believe it's better to take the time to truly enjoy your journey and appreciate your development rather than landing a rapid breakthrough. As slow and boring as it might sound, organic career growth built through a sustainable business model with strong foundations provides a lot more stability in the long term, and that's what we're looking for.

## The main investment: time

Forming a successful long-standing creative business takes time and patience, and putting in the hours is the only way to build the foundations of a strong and sustainable creative business. It takes time to perfect your skills, to press every button, to turn things upside down and look at them from a new angle, to break things and put them back together, and to get your hands dirty over and over again. Only time will help you understand who you are as a creative and why you want to do this thing for a living. Experience is the only way to truly understand the ins and outs of how the industry works, how to deal with clients, how to build resilience, how to create a reasonable work/life balance, how to sort out your taxes, and how to grow your business.

In other words, creativity takes time, but building it into a business takes even longer.

## Battling negativity

While your feel and your fuel can encourage you to get started and make the most of your ideas, you still need the right kind of motivation from yourself and your loved ones along the way. The reason being, it's almost impossible to build a creative business if you're not cheerleading yourself, or if you're surrounded by people who put you down.

This might be surprising, but you may be the first obstacle that gets in the way of your progress. Indeed, the advice to "get out of your own way" has become a cliche for a reason! Maybe you're holding yourself back from making the leap because you're telling yourself you don't have what it takes. Or perhaps you're keeping yourself in a nightmare job and daydreaming about doing something better for the soul, but telling yourself you don't deserve to live that dream instead.

If it's not ourselves, then sadly, it's sometimes the people who are closest to us who can let us down the most, especially when it comes to following our wildest dreams. Maybe they doubt you and your ambition out of love, as they worry about the impact that such a big change might have on family life, or they worry that it might not work out how you imagined and leave you disappointed (and unemployed). Or, perhaps your relatives from previous generations still carry more traditional views about what is and isn't a 'real job'.

Either way, you need to find cheerleaders who encourage you to pursue your goals. Hearing about what might go wrong, or the worst-possible-case scenarios, can be draining, but don't let that throw you off-course. Shutting off the negative noise from outside and within will help you focus on getting your creative business going. If starting a creative business feels right to you, and you're armed with the right insights, then as Dory says, "Just keep swimming!" Don't look sideways, and don't look back, no matter what your negative inner voice or the naysayers are muttering under their breath. And if you're doubting yourself right now, then as the saying goes, "Fake it till you make it!" (Which you will, I don't doubt it).

## Think and act like the person you want to become

At the start of your path, you'll need to choose a label to represent what you do. Today, you can be 'someone' or 'something' as quick as you can click 'edit settings' on an online profile. That second, you can start reaching out to people armed with your new, self-appointed title. These days, you can be anything, anytime. In fact, you can make up any title you want, and no one will give a crap.

Of course, if you do so, the problem might be that no one has the faintest idea of what you actually do. You're not a Digital Marketing Manager — you're a Conversation Architect! You're not working with the Brand Manager but the Brand Warrior, and you're not reporting to the Head of HR but the Chief People Pleaser, who reports in to the CEO, who is now called the Chief

Ninja. As painful as these are to read, they're all real-life examples! A bit like we considered earlier with the labels of 'freelancer', 'self-employed', and the like, it's helpful to pick a title that people will actually understand and that actually represents what you do.

The funny thing is that when it comes to actual, comprehensible job titles (such as developer or social media manager), it's worth remembering that many titles we wouldn't blink an eye at today didn't exist just a few decades or even years ago. And while the world is in rapid, constant flux, the need to label what we do is most likely going to be ever-present. Partly because they help others understand what we do, and partly because they help us understand what we do. Depending on your relationship to your work, your title may be worn with pride or used simply for practical purposes, like applying for freelance jobs or creating your necessary LinkedIn profile. But ultimately, they become part of your identity.

In fact, the way you view your job title in relation to your identity can be a vital indicator of how to best build a creative business around it. This means you should choose it wisely, as to some extent, it's at the heart of your business. While it might sometimes feel as though you're actually the administrator, social media exec, accountant, and chief tea maker, remember that your job title as a creative is the heart of your passion, and you should wear it with pride, even if it feels like you spend less time doing that role than the many other roles you will inevitably take on as a business owner.

## Live and breathe what you want to do

Arguably, when you're starting out, your shiny self-appointed title is more important than a new website or a decent accountant as it's often the thing you'll lead with when meeting and making future clients, collaborators, or customers, so make sure you pick something you will happily wear with pride and confidence.

And make sure it's a label you want to live and breathe. You're finally able to pursue something that you've likely dreamed about for a while, and it should be hugely exciting, so go and shout it from the rooftops. Tell everyone who you are now and what you do; call your family, message your friends, update your online profiles and social media. Because this is what you do now (even though you've got a way to go before it'll sort out your retirement fund).

Naturally, this label might feel a bit foolish when you meet a seasoned pro in your field who has many years of experience and proven track record behind them: after all, they've earned the label and grown into their profession. You might be armed with little more than bags of enthusiasm and a freshly printed business card, if even that, and this might make people question your experience, skills, and knowledge, but remember that everyone started somewhere; everyone had to fake it before they made it, to some extent.

So, wake up every morning, say your new title out loud, and do your thing. There's no time better than now, as they say. There's also no set amount of time that it takes to fully grow into your 'thing': the key is to continue evolving your mindset, and believing in who you are and what you can do.

Then, a day will come when you no longer need to tell everyone what you do now. People will know who you are as your actions will have been visible for a while, and the fruits of your labour will be there to see in plain sight.

For now, get to work every morning. That's how you earn your title. That's how you validate it for you and for everyone around you.

## I do(n't) know what I'm doing

Of course, on your journey, there will be times when you don't know what you're doing. Everyone has times where they'll readily admit they have no idea what they're doing. Life constantly throws us new challenges that have to be solved afresh.

There are also situations where you don't want to be told that someone doesn't know what they're doing. A pilot giving a tannoy announcement, for instance, or in surgery for an operation, when you've already been anaesthetised. Thankfully, the creative industry is one of the very few places where you can plead your ignorance and you might even get a round of applause. It's not a dealbreaker; in fact, for many insiders, it's the opposite.

There are endless examples of when experienced creative professionals got it wrong, and probably endless examples of where projects were more 'happy accident' than planning. Learning that it's sometimes more about luck than judgement can be very encouraging for newbie creatives. There are many variables that influence the outcome of any finished creative work.

There's no set process or formula, as it depends on a combination of everything from budgets to time to the physical environment, and even the weather when it comes to shooting photography on a set outdoors.

However, this isn't to suggest that it's always a good idea to shout about not knowing what you're doing. If you're invested in your career and genuinely passionate about what you do, you should strive to know what you're doing to the best of your ability and be able to demonstrate this to clients. Going into a meeting and telling the room that you're not really sure how things are done will not land you the project.

In other words, being a new creative professional involves a balance of knowing and accepting that there are things you can't know. People take on projects that they haven't got a clue how to execute every day, and they can make it work when they know how to join the dots and are prepared to dig deep to find the answers they need — this is all part of the process and an essential part of personal growth. However, creatives should never stop striving to know or better their craft, sharpen their skills, and expand their knowledge and expertise — this is also an essential part of personal growth. This lesson is one that I learned in a somewhat unconventional way, through starting a band...

### Growth can happen in mysterious ways

Let me set the scene. I was a fresh-faced teenager living on a sonic diet of the most amazing music arriving from every direction, and perhaps unsurprisingly, it didn't take me long to develop the idea to form my own band with some of my more musically inclined friends. We were scrappy kids, and we were on a mission to play a gig as soon as we could, and somehow, I scrambled enough cash together to buy a second-hand bass guitar. Our target interest was centred around a specific genre — death metal — which didn't require too many honed skills to get the approval of an often very drunk audience. We looked to the top of the genre for our inspiration and neglected pretty much everything else on the musical spectrum. Somehow, we did well, our tracks were pretty good, and it was a feeling like no other.

When a friend of the family, a locally renowned jazz musician, suggested that I come and collect some educational notebooks with scales and exercises, you can imagine how much I was put off by the prospect. At this point, I should probably point out that I was only fifteen. Did I really want to spend hours learning basic scales that were nowhere near what I actually wanted to play with my band? So, like an on-brand teenager, I agreed the time and date to show up, then I never did. When suggestions followed to learn classic hard rock tunes, or blues covers, or whatever else might serve as musical education, my response was that I didn't want to 'waste' my time.

Now, you can probably see where I went wrong in neglecting my musical history, but it took me a while to start analysing song structures, melodies, and scales logic to inform me of the very basic foundation of music. At some point, much later, I realised that every generation has a distinct era — with a particular fashion, architectural style, range of drugs, shape of vehicles, and musical soundtrack to daily life — and it's sometimes easy (especially when you're fifteen) to forget that past decades had their own distinct features. Every decade is now enshrined in the vast catalogue of music that defines that time, and this catalogue is full of lessons for those who are willing to listen and learn.

You can see the origins of our creativity as the ultimate cover band analogy. By applying our own personality and expression, we can create our unique version of creativity. Our creativity choices, rhythm, timing, and delivery make us unique. However, it is part of our journey to make ourselves familiar with what was here before us, to determine how it shapes us, and to realise how emulating it can aid our future progress.

When we look at the available 12 notes, full colour spectrum, or letters of the alphabet, we can sometimes feel that our choices are limited. The truth is very much the opposite. They are just the building blocks, just the beginning.

## Self-taught or formal education?

Speaking of music, how often do you hear a song that stops you in your tracks and makes you frantically find out what it is there and then (what did we do before the Shazam app!)? It's about a feeling, and one you want to experience again. Unless the song is arresting because of its creators flexing some virtuoso-level skills, you probably didn't give a second thought to the artistry behind it. How often do you wonder if that artist has an MA to their name, or if they're a Grade 8 on piano?

While early years education is a necessity, lifelong learning is, or should be, a joy. Striving to perfect your craft is a must for the longevity and creative freedom that gives you space and capacity to explore new ideas, whether that is through formal education or self-teaching, and both are fine.

In fact, I would argue that it's not about where you do the learning that matters. Think about it this way. Many people spend their degree years honing their ability to hammer their student loan and living it up away from home for the first time. Others religiously attend each class and join every society in the hope that it will set them up for their future career. But the reality is that those in the creative industries who emerge from formal education with exceptional knowledge and skills aren't necessarily the ones who paid the most attention (and usually not the ones who partied the hardest, let's be honest); it's the ones who worked really hard, putting in the time and effort to get ahead and set themselves apart.

Unfortunately, creative companies often hire those with the quantifiable skills they think they need, rather than those who can demonstrate the ability to problem-solve creatively. That part is often ring-fenced for those at the top of the food chain. Even so, it's your responsibility to look after your life-long education and to keep up to date with the skills you need. The world is moving forward fast, and it won't be stopping for you to catch up.

## Being a shapeshifting creative

As the world keeps moving, so will you. If something doesn't feel right for you in terms of your career, don't get stuck on it. When you're working for yourself, you can just move on. If your self-appointed title doesn't work anymore, or doesn't fit, you can change it.

So far in my 20-year career, I've had the opportunity to try many different creative titles and turn them into a fully-fledged career and a different way of advancing my business. My interest in graphic design led me to exploring digital illustration within my design work, so much so that I added another title, illustrator, to my name and grew to be a commercial illustrator in advertising for nearly a decade. I still worked with my design clients and explored creativity across typography and font design, but I also got to direct a couple of music videos, build countless websites and online stores, and produce motion graphics. The bottomless well of creative options was my playground for all of that time, and it still is. I believe that one's interest in creativity doesn't run out in life.

We often just find a natural end to a certain phase in our life. I no longer call myself an illustrator, but we still produce heaps of illustrations within my branding studio. I am no longer the person doing the illustration work, but I am still involved in its direction and production. There were many reasons why I made this change: for the love of work, to have more time with my family, to work directly with our clients with a much shorter decision process in the middle, and to give new talent from around the world a chance to collaborate on our projects.

It might sound like a nightmare to spend years building a name for yourself only to spend minutes reconfiguring your job title or business' focus to change lanes. However, I've seen first-hand that you can learn something from every experience, so no experience is wasted. Sometimes, things don't work out, and not every experience is going to be positive. The proverbial shit is definitely going to hit the proverbial fan, repeatedly. But since my spectacularly failed first start, my creative career and my business have taken on many different forms and variations, and I have welcomed and gained something from every single change of direction. And I promise, you will too if you have the right mindset.

## Being the odd one out

The point I've been making, in case I wasn't obvious enough, is that you will keep going, growing, learning, and hopefully earning. It's a process.

As a child, and in our formative years, we crave acceptance and hate being the odd one out. We follow the trends because we want to be 'normal' and make others keep their pointing fingers firmly in their pockets.

It takes time to get comfortable in our own skin. How long it takes to feel content in ourselves differs for everyone, but we start to embrace our uniqueness as our confidence grows. Generally speaking, we become more outgoing, and lean into our eccentricities, as we get older. With age comes the realisation that for all of our worrying about what everyone else thinks, they're only really thinking about themselves for the most part. Over time, we strengthen our resilience — and we give a lot less of a shit about how everyone else perceives us and what others might be thinking.

In other words, we come to embrace our personality and our style of expression, and this often happens organically as we get older. Still, it can take time and courage to become someone who stands out, and if you want to turbo-charge the rate of this happening, then work on embracing what makes you 'you'.

This can seem obvious in careers such as show business, where celebrities have people helping them to dial up their uniqueness for their public persona. To a regular mortal, it might seem exhausting for musicians, performers, or actors to be dressed up to the nines all the time. However, being the odd one out and standing out with a memorable or quickly distinguishable image is just part of their job description. Wearing dresses made out of meat, sporting oversized eccentric glasses, or strutting about in a big, furry jacket is often a ticket to get noticed and therefore get publicity.

Celebrities dress up to be memorable. Rich people dress up to show off their wealth. Creatives can or should dress up to show off their brand of creativity. What I mean is, these things are just an exercise to stand out as a creative, and you can fast-track this by focusing on what makes you unique, then it's easier to be recognised for that and build your brand of creativity around it (though maybe avoid the meat dress and snazzy glasses).

### Being an alien

**Alien** - *(noun)*
*A person who does not belong to a particular family, community, country, etc.; a foreigner, a stranger, an outsider.* [Oxford English Dictionary]

For some people, being the 'odd one out' is more a matter of circumstance, because their skin colour, accent, or birth name can make them seem unusual. When you're starting a new business, the world is your oyster, as they say, which means you might choose to set it up somewhere away from home. Starting a new career in a different country or speaking a different language might seem like making things especially difficult, especially if it's without the safety of friends and family. However, this shouldn't mean you shouldn't try it if it's what you've got your heart set on.

The reason why cosmopolitan cities like London or New York flourish is down to the fact they're so multicultural, as the diversity of thinking and talent from different people create a tapestry of experiences that drives innovation and creativity.

Many immigrants forging careers in new countries find that being far from home brings them extra focus and energy. While local people might talk about the enhanced work ethic of those who come from overseas, immigrants often just see it as a need to build safety nets to ensure they keep moving forward.

I know this because I've worked in the creative industry for 21 years, and I've lived in a different country to the one I was born in for the last 23 years. During those years, I've experienced my fair share of negative opinions being thrown my way; my somewhat confusing name has been assumed to originate from many different countries; my accent has been scrutinised. For the first 5 to 10 years, I was the subject of casual racism.

And so for a long time, I did all I could to be as inconspicuous as possible. Now, I truly don't care what some narrow-minded people might think. I focus on my family, my work and life. And

I also noticed that a lot of the negative things happened less as I got older, as I got bolder in my work and processes, and as I got bolder as a person. Being an alien can be both an advantage and a disadvantage until you reach the point when you and your work are so good that no one can ignore you.

Whether it's moving abroad or something else, the lesson is that those who want an easy ride in life don't push outside their own walls, but this is why extra challenges come with extra sweet rewards. If moving away is the right path for you, then embrace the challenge.

## The uneven starting line

You're almost ready to get started, so I have one thing left to say on the matter: there's no such thing as an equal footing when it comes to starting out.

When someone jumps into their own small business right after finishing their studies, their contact book is going to be filled with blank pages, and their industry knowledge starts from zero. If starting a creative business is one of the first things you're looking to do after education, ask yourself whether you have the necessary experience right now. If the answer is no, then it might be a good idea to join a company in a relevant field for a few years before you go solo. There's always value in seeing how business works in terms of project delivery, client liaison, and the intricacies of business.

For someone going solo after a decade in industry, they've had time to build up their skills and make contacts. And that's why, in my opinion, there's no such thing as starting a creative business too late. So many independent artists and makers have rebuilt their life around a decision to pursue their creative calling. Starting this journey later in life can give you the benefit of wider experience, broader knowledge, and hindsight to build upon, not to mention the greater reserves of patience. A later start might also mean that you have a better financial safety net. The calmness that comes with age and experience often means that people know what needs to be done to cover the distance. However, will you be looking at your employment years wishing you jumped solo sooner?

Ultimately, neither setup is better than the other — if you're prepared for the challenge — and the starting line will even out over time. Either way, you need the same things to get started.

**How do I get started?**
Make a plan. Set a start date. Stick to it.
Tell a friend or partner about your plan. Become accountable.
Remember that even a failed start is a good start.
Do it right and it will last.

**What do I need?**
Plenty of fuel and feel.
Your magic formula and your superpower
Generosity. Emotional intelligence. Intrigue.
And a pinch of creativity...

... which is enough to keep you coming back for more.

"Our business in life is not to get ahead of others, but to get ahead of ourselves."

E. Joseph Cossman

Creativity for Sale

Pages

# 72—95

# Chapter - no.3
# Define

Chapter - no.3

# 77. Why define?
# 78. *Being uniquely yourself*
# 80. Define your what and how
# 81. *Define your personal brand statement*
# 81. Define your skill stack
# 82. *Define your values*
# 84. Define your niche

85. *Define your reach*
86. Define your expectations
87. Define your goals
89. *What is 'enough'?*
90. What is success?
91. *What is your personal best?*

Creativity for Sale

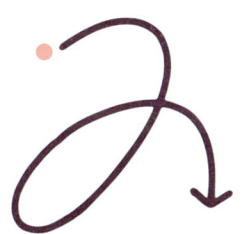

This chapter will show you how to take your magic formula and turn it into a business. You'll look at your direction and abilities, then compare them to your own expectations and vision. A lot of creatives chase impossible targets that are defined by others, not by themselves, but following others rather than being true to yourself will only make you feel unsatisfied. That's why this chapter is about you defining what works for you.

## Why define?

Successful artists and entrepreneurs usually share one trait: they've defined where they're heading in the long term, what they're roughly planning to achieve on their journey, and what the final outcome will ideally look like. That's how they turn their dream into a strategy.

On the other hand, there are also plenty of creatives who

think about today and spare little thought about tomorrow, and it is perfectly possible to aimlessly bumble along and still make a good job of it. There are, no doubt, many creatives who can attest to having succeeded in their career without a personal manifesto and roadmap.

It depends what you want the journey to look like. Imagine two people trying to get from A to B. The first person has a map and clear directions of which roads to take to reach their destination in the easiest, quickest way. The second simply gets told where they're expected to end up, but they have no map and no directions — just a basic idea of the landscape around them. The second person is guaranteed to take a lot longer, and to take a fair few wrong turns on the way.

Of course, getting lost can be really fun, and I speak from experience when I say that. But sometimes, when we look back at the past, we wish we'd taken more control over our decisions, and that regret can override the joyful memories of past experiences. This is why I'd argue that you should have an idea of where you're going and how you're going to get there, even if it's just for a little while. There's still plenty of room to take detours and enjoy the scenery, and you might find that where you wanted to end up changes over time, but at least you're heading in the right direction. So, let's start gathering a map of sorts.

## Being uniquely yourself

In a world where you could be anyone and anything, what do you want to bring to the table?

Define

The biggest artists are uniquely themselves, just think about musicians, artists, fashion designers, or creatives that you admire, or even better, worship. These people consistently take their magic formula and use their superpower to build their unique brand of creativity. That's why we are fully aware of their approach, identity, and purpose. They're visible thanks to their uniqueness and how it's been dialled up for everyone to see. This chapter will help you formulate why you deserve to be seen by people too.

When you're being your true self, you rid yourself of competition. Instead, you gain peers and contemporaries, fans, and some inevitable enemies too. When the world can see your why, how, and what, they naturally feel interested to work with you. As such, defining your brand is an essential personal marketing exercise.

Although it's tempting to ignore this process and get knocking on people's doors to find work right away, it'll only make your future efforts more difficult as you will find it hard to cut through the noise if you look and sound like everybody else.

Of course, it can feel difficult to articulate your core offering to an audience of possible clients or prospective customers. So, start asking yourself some questions, like:

What is it you do exactly? Why should people work with you and not someone else? What is your unique set of skills and knowledge? Why are you the right solution to their problem?

One thing is guaranteed here — you will tweak the answers to these questions as your business takes shape.

Every brand adapts and changes to survive, so never stick with a plan that doesn't work just because you made a plan.

## Define your what and how

Your **'what'** is about defining the size and shape of the problem you're going to solve.

- What pain points are you going to remove?
- What problem are you going to solve for people?
- What skill set is currently in demand?
- What do you know about the current technology in your industry that can be invaluable to other companies?

In the world of business, the 'what' is your main objective. The 'what' can change, but it's you who provides it, and this gives you the ability to adapt to change when it's needed.

Your **'how'** is the way you offer your 'what'.
This is often about the practicalities of how you will work.

- Will you work directly or indirectly?
- On-site or remote? In-person or online?
- Will you work on your own, as part of a team, or lead your own team of collaborators or suppliers?

In other words, how do you connect and deliver your skill set to your clients?

### Define your personal brand statement

Now, let's bring this together. Summarise your brand personality, creative philosophy, and other important points in one simple line that will help you articulate what you do to anyone.

Your personal brand statement is meant to be short and to the point. It should simply introduce you, what you do, and what you work on. Spelling it out in economical, precise language makes it far easier to see the road ahead.

Try the following format to get started, and tweak it as many times as you need to arrive at a version you're happy with:

*I am (name + title or profession) who does (what problem do you solve) with (your clientele or audience) for (outcome) by doing (your unique selling point)*

*For example: I am Radim Malinic, a branding creative director who turns ideas into brands of the future. I work with start-ups and established brands to create exciting products through engaging visual storytelling.*

### Define your skill stack

Your skill stack is a jigsaw of many pieces of experience, skills, and traits, and these often go beyond your core offering or product. In fact, the skills you pick up on your career and life journey start from a young age, and there's a lot you can already do with your magic formula and superpower, and there's also a lot you can add to your skill stack. Indeed, there's never a time when you've collected too many skills or too much knowledge.

Realistically, it takes time to build your creative skill stack, learn the fundamentals of business, and finesse your processes, and it can even be a lifelong journey. But the longer you practise this myriad of skills, the better you should get across the board as a creative professional.

A broader skill stack can give you an advantage in solving bigger problems, having more elaborate conversions with collaborators, elevating your output beyond its borders, and making you more adaptable to what the future might bring.

You already started defining your skill stack earlier with your magic formula and superpower, but this shouldn't be a one-and-done exercise. You may not need to keep a formal CV now you've escaped the corporate, employed world, but you should still keep a record of your skills, experiences, and knowledge to keep track of your skill stack yourself and have a plan for your future learning.

## Define your values

Now it's time to get bigger. Your values are what you consider to be the most important things in life, in business, and in relationships. Over the course of time, as you become more experienced in these areas, your personal, creative, and business values are likely to change.

Our younger selves are often busy drinking a confusing cocktail of outside influences, but as we grow, we start to notice what we align with and what we don't.

In our early days, our creative values are often inward-facing, meaning we are on the path to prove ourselves. First, we have to prove to ourselves that we can do what we've set out to do. Then, we have to prove to others that we can deliver the work that's needed of us.

As such, our **inward-looking** values might be:
— **Focus**: caring about detail and delivery
— **Passion**: striving to do the best possible work
— **Innovation**: being curious to do something different

There is nothing wrong with such a mindset, of course. If you're driven to be the best version of yourself, then this will naturally lead to a focus on your own skill set and achievements, and your values won't extend much into the outside world, at least not for now.

This isn't a bad thing. It's just your vision. People will see that you bring your A game everywhere you go, and they will totally buy into what you have to offer. They will see your 'why' and it will help them make the right decision whether to work with you. They will understand that your value is to deliver great work that goes beyond their expectations.

Once you've been around the block a few times, your values will start to shift with your view of the world, and they will become more outward-looking. You will start to care less about what you get from the process and more about what you give to enrich others with your creativity. This doesn't mean that your original values are no longer valid or are obsolete — it simply means that you build on top of those values and add extra layers.

Your updated values will include the reasons why your creativity can serve a greater purpose than just hitting your personal best.

Your **outward-looking** values might be:
— **Trust**: Being trustworthy and accountable, and having integrity
— **Dedication**: Wanting to make a difference through your creativity
— **Sustainability**: Caring about the environment and your impact on it
— **Generosity**: Helping people to achieve their goals with the tools you provide

### Define your niche

Now let's get narrow. Having a niche or style, even a temporary one, is an asset in finding the right message and offering for a specific group of people. If you do 'everything for everyone', you certainly won't get bored anytime soon, but in the long term, it's tricky to establish a foundation of repeat work, and it's impossible to reach the attention of everyone, so it makes your marketing even more time-consuming and expensive. If you try to appeal to everyone, you will most likely end up reaching no one.

Your niche offering or artistic style can be your main asset and the focus of your marketing messaging, but this doesn't mean you're restricted to doing just that. You can always keep your mind curious and your skill set evolving as you work across other disciplines or projects behind the scenes. Then, in the very likely event of markets and demands shifting, you may already be ahead of the curve with your secret skills, or you might have developed a new style that is more likely to command attention in a changed world.

For now, make it simple for yourself and those who wish to find you. Focus on one thing that will define your niche or style, and it will serve you just right. Identify the group of people, brands, and companies that are most likely in need of what you can offer. Now, zoom in on where they are and how to find them.

## Define your reach

It's easy to dream about having worldwide reach, having a business that truly transcends all continents and nations. But… the reality could prove a bit more challenging. A creative service thrives on personal recommendations and collaborations. So, when you start thinking about your reach, always start at or near wherever you're based. That way, you can see first-hand how your community works. You already know the people who might use your service upon introduction or recommendation. This is where it all begins.

I am a firm believer, from experience, that making meaningful connections will provide you with the best circumstances for work collaborations and business growth. The more personal connections are often the ones that last the longest and offer the most fruitful outcomes.

Of course, there's no limit to where your journey might take you (as I explained in the previous chapter), but bear in mind that while the creative industry prides itself on multiculturalism, the nuances of local cultures and traditions are often complex, and it's rare that you can achieve global appeal and harmony alone. If you're working globally, it may be worth having local service providers who can handle the work delivery, client liaison, and any parts in between.

And while being able to work with clients across the globe is a thrilling prospect, only by establishing yourself in a local setting first will you build the strong foundations you need to reach further afield.

## Define your expectations

What do you want? Big budget projects? Legions of fans? A style that inspires a cult following? Something that everyone will love? Fame and fortune? A mansion or a campervan?

Your expectations should be led by certain criteria, like how many other people have the exact same skills as you? How many people work in the same style? Is your work seasonal or will you be busy all year round? How can your magic formula give you a unique place in the market? What is your realistic earning per piece of work or project? Your expectations should also be led by a dose of realism.

By defining your expectations and being realistic about the possibilities that lie ahead, you will create a clearer picture of how to build your business. You can see how others in a similar position made it work and think about what you might have to compromise on. Also remember that your expectations will change with experience. If you struggle to set the right benchmarks, seek out an industry peer or established professional who can help you set the most realistic view of what's to come. They were most likely in the same position of lacking clarity when they started.

## Define your goals

Many people in life have goals, though arguably, many of them don't succeed in making those goals happen. Some people have goals that are defined by societal behaviour, like owning a house, buying a nice car, living in a safe area, and going on this or that impressive holiday. People may also have personal goals for various parts of their life, like eating well, being good at tennis, writing a book, making a movie, or falling in love. Then there are people who don't have goals and would argue that life can be enjoyed without having moving targets to hit. In fact, it may be an easier way to live without the added pressure, effort, or disappointment of trying to constantly achieve things. Or in other words, a goal that doesn't exist won't keep you up at night.

Of course, some people can spend a career lifetime without setting goals and still achieve a fair bit, like a few job promotions, a few projects that worked out nicely, and some fond memories. Even when running a small business, it's possible to look back and realise you've spent a considerable amount of time without many celebrated wins because you didn't have goals. There's nothing wrong with that, but it makes the rear-view mirror a lot less exciting to look at.

A defined goal gives you a purpose, and it can turn inertia into energy, and that's one of the many reasons why I advocate having goals to aim for in your business. The problem is that when it comes to running a creative business, goals can easily be mistaken for a list of dream clients or brands, and they rarely have any actions attached to make these dreams happen. Since this means that things are largely left to chance, those goals are unlikely to ever be reached.

The truth is: some business goals will be met. Some will get scrapped. Minds will be changed. Sometimes, despite having a defined goal, we may be unable to make any progress; however, most of our realistic goals can be achieved, and it relies on continual resilience and determination over the course of time. Goals aren't meant to be easy, although a low-hanging fruit always tastes nice, right?

A goal of this book is to get your creative business up and running, and that's why every page details the practical actions needed to achieve it. If you lack a practical framework to achieve your goal, the end result isn't going to happen, and the goal is still just a dream. What's more, the framework gives you the metrics to check whether you're getting there and alert you when you've finally achieved it, and that definitely tastes better in the long-term than low-hanging fruit.

## What is 'enough'?

When you get very good at putting goals and systems in place, the results can inspire you to put further ideas into action. It might feel as though the next logical step is to pursue more ideas that will help you progress more in your professional or personal life. Ticking off goals one by one is a great motivator to tick off more.

However, having too many goals might produce negative emotional and even physical outcomes. When your creative business onboards more clients than you ever dreamed of, you have to ramp up production to meet all of their needs and requirements, which can lead to overworking and burnout. When things go well, you start seeing financial rewards; you have more in the bank than you thought possible, so what's your next move? Cap the incoming work or reach for more?

The lack of a clear 'enough' is often the driver behind growing teams or expanding business locally and internationally. Sometimes, that's a positive thing, but likewise, it can have the opposite effect and make a business overcommit or lose its focus.

Everyone's 'enough' looks different. If you fail to define what is enough for you, you can end up back on the open road, with multiple stops but no end destination. Impatience is a very human quality, and we often want to sprint towards our career goals by chasing creative work, pursuing every new idea, getting tons of new clients, and producing as much work as possible to make a name for ourselves. But, remember that it's impossible to sprint a whole marathon, and having no defined goals or career checkpoints can turn into an endless race without any reward.

When it's your business, the only person you're running against is yourself, so take it at a pace that works for you, take regular breaks to check in with yourself and your plan, and make sure you're still on course for where you want to go.

## What is success?

For some people, 'enough' is defined as success. Sure, success is good for the soul, and it can be the ultimate driver as it's the outcome of purpose, values, and action. But again, what 'success' means to you needs to be defined.

Success might be found in **inward-facing** things like:
— Having the space to grow as a person.
— Waking up and wanting to do the same thing you did yesterday.
— Having a calm mind in the middle of the storm.
— Living your own life story.
— The courage to deal with failure and keep going back for more until it works.

Success might be **outward-facing** things like:
— Creating something that makes someone smile.
— Telling a story that makes someone feel something.
— Making the first ripple in a chain reaction of inspiration.
— Being able to share your generosity.
— Knowing that what you do is making a difference in someone's life.

Success might be **practical** things like:
— Having £1 left in the bank after you've paid all of the suppliers, taxes, bills, and life expenses. Having £1m left in the bank account after you've paid everything.
— Making something out of nothing.
— Not needing an employed job.
— Knowing you've got enough to make you happy.

While I mentioned a few metrics of success that relate to finances, I want to make it clear that your entire idea of success shouldn't revolve around money. Think about what you want to achieve for yourself, not just what you think other people might measure success against, or what might look like success on social media.

### What is your personal best?

When you run a small company, you will most likely, at some point along the path, find yourself juggling sales and marketing, client meetings, project delivery, future-proofing, staff management, payroll, and anything else you can imagine. All of this can leave very little space for you to grow to be your best creatively. It can also leave very little room for you to notice your progression, or lack thereof. The people who will eventually end up working for you full time will no doubt grow in some ways, but if a creative employee feels overlooked or even invisible, they can begin to feel resentful and undervalued, and it won't be long before they're looking for a new role.

I was in that situation for the first four years of my career. Neither of my two full-time roles required special skills to deliver the mid-level work required. That was great in some ways as I was a graphic designer who could explore many different styles for vastly different business sectors, with no key performance indicators and a fairly loose creative process.

On one hand, this was the right playground to get first-hand experience of how creative work should and shouldn't be conducted. As long as the work was done and the invoices were paid, everyone seemed happy, the leadership team was busy counting their profits, and no one really cared how much better the whole operation could have been or took the time to invest in making each person more brilliant with extra help and guidance. On the other hand, there was a lack of development opportunities, and my growth was stifled, like a plant kept in the dark.

Rather than seek another employed role, my desire to grow led me to build my freelance business after work hours, often long into the dead of night when I sacrificed sleep to improve my creative skills. Working directly with clients in this way enabled me to pursue ideas much further than in my 9–5, as there was more room for exploratory creativity and improvement.

My hunger grew, and I wanted to create work that was technically better, imagining how much better the final outcome could be if I applied myself and strived to improve overall. Around that time, I came across *It's Not How Good You Are, It's How Good You Want to Be* by Paul Arden.

Even though I was aware of so many more talented people than me, that book encouraged me to set out on my own journey, which would see me finding the best version of myself.

Ultimately, I realised that even if my employers didn't care whether I was becoming my best self, I really did care. Whatever stage you're at — employee, freelancer, or small business owner — you should always take the time to define what you're personally striving for. That way, you're more likely to feel fulfilled and proud of yourself. And when you're a small business owner with employees, you should take the time to help them define what their personal best is too. That way, they're less likely to ditch you for another employed role or their own hustle.

There's no need to seek outside metrics to define how good you want to be. Only you can decide that. Growth starts from within, and it's a lifelong journey.

This is your power of one.

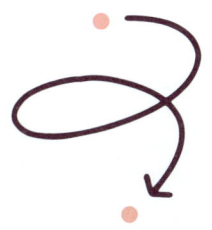

Creativity for Sale

"Give me six hours to chop down a tree and I will spend the first four sharpening the axe."

Abraham Lincoln

Creativity for Sale

Pages
96—117

## Chapter - no.4
# Build

Creativity for Sale

Chapter - no.4

**101.** Understanding brand and identity
**103.** *Understanding market research*
**103.** Choose your name
**105.** *Consider trademarking*
**106.** Build your unique identity
**108.** *Build your branded assets*

**108.** Build your portfolio
**110.** *Is social media the be-all-and-end-all?*
**112.** That doesn't include LinkedIn
**114.** *The power of email*
**115.** Consider business stationery
**116.** *Choose your wardrobe*

Creativity for Sale

In the last chapter, you started to define yourself and your offering, formulating the vision and strategy of your business, and you learned that this is an ongoing process. Even though you might have what feels like the most brilliant creative idea ever, making it work is the only way you can get proof of that concept, and that means you need to build a brand. That's why in this chapter, we'll start building your creative brand by creating the assets that support these things, because building a strong brand is vital to the success of any business in the long term. So, get your toolbox and let's start building.

## Understanding brand and identity

The notion of a 'brand' originally came from the unique mark burned onto livestock so their owners could identify them. Now, a brand more commonly means a uniquely distinguishable company, or in smaller terms, a unique product, service, or concept offered by a company. In other words, it's what makes your company your company as opposed to another company.

Your brand is what people see of your business, and this is why people often think of branding as things like your company name, logo, colour palette, and type of images (your visuals). But it's also much broader than that as it's about how people connect and interact with you (such as your website and social media), and about your style of working and advertising yourself. These are the different layers of branding.

Having more layers to your branding means that people have more to identify with, and it gives them more information about who and what your business is about. Branding is ultimately about trust, and something that people perceive as trustworthy can usually command higher prices. However, you don't have to emulate other people or businesses' approaches to branding, as you can create your own version with whatever you feel is the right mixture to build your brand and reputation. Like do you want to do talks on the speaking circuit and get interviewed on podcasts? Or would you rather let your work do the talking? Both of these methods can be equally effective and suit different types of people.

Either way, if you get your business' branding right for you and your target clients, then you open the door to opportunities. By contrast, if you leave your branding up to chance or what others think you should do, then you'll spend more time chasing work than doing it, and you'll have a hard time convincing people that you're the right one to take that work on.

## Understanding market research

To build your brand, you need to start with market research, which is essentially a fancy way of saying 'looking at who's already doing what you're planning to do'. As I mentioned earlier, it's easy to think that the whole world should be your potential clients, but even established brands can't appeal to everyone, let alone a one-man band, or one-man brand. That's why I recommend starting local. Search engines are often the best jumping-off point for market research here, as you'll need to know who provides the same service in your area. Then you can broaden the search to your region, and then to the wider country.

First, make a shortlist of those you see as direct competitors as they provide the same service in the same place and price bracket (if you've determined what your price bracket is). Note the exact services they offer, the sort of problems they're solving, their visual brand identity (name, colours, fonts, imagery, photography style), their previous work, and how many people are in their team (if they are a studio or even an agency rather than an individual).

Then make another shortlist of the non-competitors who you aspire to be as good as. This is your 'moonshot list', which will benchmark your own brand. The reason for having a moonshot list is because you're going to attempt to improve your overall ambition and reach higher in your pool of competitors.

## Choose your name

Once you've done your research, you can start zooming in

on your own brand, which often starts with your brand name. There are different types of brand names, from traditional and authority-inducing ones like *'Chris Tucker from Tucker and Partners'* to fun, one-word names like *'Beeple'*, or more modern compound names like *'RaggedEdge'* or phrases like *'Brand Nu'*. Think about what type of brand name is best suited to what you do.

But before you choose a name and start designing your assets, bear in mind that you ideally want it to be as memorable or even unique as possible, which is a challenge in itself these days considering the number of businesses in existence. You'll need to check whether any companies have registered the name already (the Companies House website shows you this in the UK), as well as the trademark register, available domain names, and social media handles.

You'll soon find that this limits your shortlist considerably, so don't be afraid to get creative. In fact, your name could be derived from the way you define your creativity, and you can make a great impression with words or an implied meaning that evokes your personal creative philosophy. Many well-known creatives simply stuck the word 'Studio' after their name, but I think you can be more creative than that. (Or you can sod the sensible naming options altogether and go for a name that's totally bonkers; it will be memorable at least. Yes, I'm looking at you Ice Cream for Free, a creative practice name that you won't forget anytime soon.)

Sounding out ideas with your friends and people in your community or network is often a useful way to get instant, honest feedback. My wife calls this 'the pub test'. If it makes sense immediately in an informal setting, you might be onto something. Next, run the 'phone test', that is, try to say 'your name + company name' as a response to an incoming call. Then try the same as an outgoing call. Does it still work? Can you say the words easily? Are people likely to understand you clearly the first time? Call your mum, or better still, your gran, and make them your unofficial focus group. If they get it, you're winning.

With any name, my advice would be to keep it simple and easy to pronounce; that way, it'll be more memorable, and easier for people to search for. Whatever their age, many people struggle with spelling. So, in my experience, the fewer keys that people have to press to load your domain in their browser, the better. Keep it short and simple.

The availability of domain names should be a consideration, but don't discount a business name just because the domain is already taken. You can pick another domain, as long as it makes sense with your business name. For example, if *brandnu.co.uk* had already been taken, I could have gone with *brandnustudio.co.uk* or *brand-nu.co.uk*.

## Consider trademarking

Once you've reached the end of the (possibly fun, possibly arduous) naming process, you might want to consider putting a trademark application in to secure your name for the future and its potential uses. You can trademark your company name, logo, product names, and more.

Trademarks are assigned in different groups, called 'classes', to allow multiple uses of the same name across different companies. For example, sports equipment brands have one class for shoes (class 25), another for glasses (009), walking sticks (18), and so forth. Each of the products falls into a different class, where the name is protected. Your creative business might expand into other products, such as clothing, software, or other activities, and they might be covered by the original class choice, like (25) also covers golf clubs.

It's worth noting that during the trademarking process, your name(s) may be disputed by another company who has a stake in protecting their name, and this is why you should check the trademark register before choosing your company name and spending a lot of money on printing any promo material or clothing. If you're unlucky here, you might have to go back to the drawing board, and that will likely be a lot of hassle. Or, it could be an opportunity to come up with something even better.

## Build your unique identity

Your public identity often isn't 'the real you', i.e., the person you are in the privacy of your own home or when hanging out with friends. You might be the person who gets a little too tipsy at weddings and starts ranting to everyone about the current state of badly kerned fonts, but your professional identity should be a little more 'curated' than that, and it should say something about the work you do, and how you do it.

The reality, as you might drunkenly tell people, is that these days, every brand is starting to look the same. In a saturated market, this is bound to happen, and everyone starts to look and sound like everybody else, across multiple industries and sectors. This is why the race is on for some companies to relaunch their brand with a more distinct identity to rise above the crowd, yet even the modern refresh of many high-profile brands, products, or start-ups is beginning to look alike.

To build a unique identity, you'll need a visual brand toolkit, consisting of a compelling logo, custom colour palette, and consistent typefaces and imagery, as these will build your brand equity and strengthen your visibility and reputation. But you will also really benefit from a suite of world-class assets, a strong presentation deck, snazzy animated visuals, a killer business card, website, and easily shared portfolio. If you want to go even further, get branded clothing featuring your brand ID or some of your visual work. The latter will work wonders in securing a more emotional and empowering connection with your personal identity and values for potential customers, your employees, and even you! (A little tip, put a QR code on the back of your shirt.)

Here, like a choose your own adventure book, you've got three choices on how to proceed:
- Do nothing and pursue your offer without any visual identity.
- Do what others do: try to emulate your chosen benchmark brand and settle there.
- Go to town and dial up whatever will make you look and sound like your best self.

Which will you choose? (Okay, the correct answer should be obvious.)

## Build your branded assets

Your suite of branded assets is arguably as important in making an impression as a specific project in your portfolio. Whether it's your project proposal, invoice, statement of work, presentation deck, or project contract, any effort to be consistently on-brand will pay dividends. I've converted quite a few client enquiries into projects thanks to my estimate document design, as it inspired the prospect to see what even the smallest part of their business could look like.

If you don't feel like spending too much time on your digital assets, there's many websites that offer ready-made templates. However, like your website design, remember any template can be purchased by countless others, and it's always better to stand out with something unique.

## Build your portfolio

Most of us are very familiar with the idea that less is more, but we have a hard time self-curating our own work accordingly. It's especially hard at the beginning, and it's easy to get carried away and want to show off everything we've done so far in the hope that whoever might need our services will find something they like enough to pick us from the pile of options.

Personally, I used to be dreadful at curating my portfolio. When I was a newbie, a friend called me with an offer to work as an assistant for an established graphic designer, and this direct recommendation could have helped me secure the spot.

When asked to send across my work, I didn't yet have a proper website or collated portfolio to highlight my strengths and signature style, so I decided to put together a folder with more than 80 pieces of totally random design work: experimental gig posters, corporate business cards, brochures, logo sketches, and some vector illustrations and mixed media collages. It was a mess, and unsurprisingly, I didn't get the job.

Although it's hard, it's vital to self-curate your portfolio and show only your best and most relevant work. Soon enough, your work will become synonymous with who you are as a creative brand. Your body of work is your visual personal brand statement, but it will also keep changing and evolving, so you should update your website and folder as you progress in your career.

If you're using your portfolio as a direct way of getting new work, you have to think and act like your potential clients.

Ask yourself:
— What do they need to see?
— How do you get them to understand your core offering?
— Where will they look to find new suitable talent for their work?
— Do you offer a particular artistic style, or do you solve problems?

The former might require a more visually rich collection to show versatility or diversity of application, while the latter requires a description of a problem-solving journey from start to finish, with supporting imagery and relevant stats that demonstrate your work's success.

A visually rich portfolio can be curated according to client or sector, or different styles of work. Alternatively, it might simply be a few case studies that detail your unique creative process. By contrast, a problem-solving portfolio should contain around six to eight project case studies. In both types of portfolio, your supporting text needs to be strong and direct, ideally 400 words per project page to showcase the logic behind the project.

Once you've gathered your portfolio content, think about the best way to present it. Many creatives start building their portfolio on a website using a premade template, which you can do and add your own branding and personality later. However, the best sites are custom-built to help you truly express your unique brand and demonstrate first-hand what you can do. Using social media as a portfolio is obviously simple, but it shouldn't be seen as an alternative to a standalone website as they're just not the same thing, and you should really have both.

A portfolio is a foundation of your toolkit as a creative business, and ultimately, your own corner of the internet, which should get your prospects focused on what you have to say and offer. The main benefit of your website is being able to track incoming traffic and seeing who is interested in what you do.

## Is social media the be-all-and-end-all?

It's pretty obvious that you need some kind of social media presence as a creative, but this can lead to the temptation to be on every platform. Put simply, you will never be able to conquer each and every social site, and unless you have deep pockets to employ a whole team of social media specialists, attempting to be active on every platform is only really for the big brands. It can also be extremely time-consuming, whether you're active on one platform or all of them.

While social media can be a great platform for storytelling, to discover fellow creatives, and forge communities, such platforms are also designed to sap as much energy and time as possible to keep you on there. They can be excellent distractions, but with the likes of Instagram and Tik Tok working on algorithms that constantly change, it feels rare these days to see new, exciting content rather than ads or sponsored posts. So, don't let researching and running these platforms overtake your work and your clients. It's easy to get consumed by social media, but a cost-effective freelancer can be a far better solution to save your precious time as a business owner.

Don't get me wrong, you can use your social media profile to be generous with your knowledge and skills, and it can gather significant followers and engagement if you get it right. However, ask yourself: Do you want to be a content creator or actually run your creative business?

If the latter, then the best way to curate and design your social media is to put yourself in your audience's shoes. What do they need to see to take action? Which content format best serves your purpose of getting them to do something? Action is key, yet I'm always surprised by the number of creatives who have no social media strategy to drive action yet expect potential customers to contact them through such platforms, and even use those same platforms to complain when people don't.

Finally, think about how your social media content can demonstrate your creative skills while also presenting your unique brand identity. Social media can be like a giant department store where we are all sat in boxes side by side on shelves, with very little nuance or deviation between our images or voices, so it can be very difficult to stand out and sometimes not worth the hassle of trying, as controversial as that might sound in today's world.

Look, I know that most people see a big social media following as imperative for a creative business's success, but when you really analyse the size of established studios and their comparable social media following, you'll soon realise that follower count doesn't really matter, as their work speaks for itself. And just like fancy brands in a high-end department store, the highest quality companies are often shrouded in an aura of intrigue and mystery anyway.

Your follower count can be great for your motivation if that's what you're into, but the ability to check your follower count and like notifications anytime can be the worst thing for your productivity if you allow it. Whatever you post, give it time and space, and let the seed grow. Check your socials daily at a specific time, and make it part of your schedule; otherwise, it will eat up all of your schedule through the constant impulsive nudge to check your social media.

### That doesn't include LinkedIn

Okay, when I said 'social media', I don't mean that all social media is built equally. While the more visual social media platforms tend to be a chaotic mix of reels, newsflashes, memes, and sponsored ads, LinkedIn is the platform that is seen as the most like a genuine workplace, which might be obvious as it's work-focused, and perhaps naturally less distracting.

However, the benefits for professionals go beyond just 'less annoying than the other platforms'. Firstly, it enables you to share views on your industry, share links to articles or news that may be beneficial to your peers, and help you appear in potential clients' feeds. In that way, LinkedIn can be a great place to find future prospects, but also bear in mind that it's just one point of contact and interaction, not the be all and end all. Plus, there is plenty of bad practice in action on the platform, especially when people or businesses see it as a marketplace to sell what they're offering, rather than a meeting place to inform and be informed, and form genuine connections.

This is not to say that you shouldn't try to find clients through LinkedIn, but it is saying that you should care about adding value to an online community, not just increase the value of your bank balance, and a focus on the latter can make you seem disingenuous. If you really want to find clients, it's worth using a specialist agency as they know the format better than anyone else, so you'll save yourself time and get the right results without annoying your followers.

In the Amplify section, we'll talk in more detail about how to make meaningful connections instead of firing off cold messages to those you have only just connected with. But for now, if you're going to add anything useful, record a short intro video with your elevator pitch, add a voice note to help people pronounce your name properly, and add some milestone projects to show people what you do. Then, focus on finding real connections.

## The power of email

In a world dominated by social media, it can be easy to forget about the power of the humble email. A branded email is another contact point that strengthens your company's image and builds trust with potential clients.

If you did the work earlier, you'll have a snappy domain name and a slick website, so don't make the mistake of still using your Gmail (or even worse, Hotmail) email address. It just doesn't look professional, especially when you can pay a little for a service that provides a matching email address to your domain name (like *hi@brandnu.co.uk*, which looks infinitely better than *brandnu@gmail.com*). As with your domain and company name, make it simple and easy to spell.

When you're dealing with bigger companies as a small creative business, you can even set up multiple 'aliases' like *admin@brandnu.co.uk*, *finance@*, *accountspayable@*, or *contact@*, even if those emails actually end up in the same inbox!

Your branded email address also needs a stellar email signature design, as it can make you look established from day one and make your message stand out in a potential client's inbox. When you get emails from bigger companies, take note of the best current practices, and if you're not signed up to any mailing lists, sign up to a few of your 'moonlist' to model what they do. This way, it's easy to spot what looks good, what looks too corporate, and what might confuse people.

Your email signature should use your branding (logo, colours, etc.) and include useful links, though refrain from adding every social media channel, even if you're active on all of them. You could add a link to a recent blog post, media feature, or project that might intrigue people. In the past, my email signature mentioned that I had a new website, as it served as a quick prompt for those making enquiries and potential clients to check out my website and offer. That 'new website' stayed in my signature for more than a year because it worked.

It's also worth having a secondary signature with fewer details and features for subsequent conversations with the client or their team. Keep tweaking the design and links as you go along.

### Consider business stationery

If we've gone back in time from social media to emails, then the mention of business stationery might seem ancient. Not that long ago, almost every business, regardless of size or industry, kept a stack of branded letterheads, compliment slips, envelopes, and business cards for every employee. But in the 21st Century, stationery can seem like an unnecessary hassle and expenditure. Why bother putting effort and money into something that has been predominantly replaced with digital touch points, right? Well, many large businesses still see the value, and business stationery does still hold validity. Even though physical correspondence has rapidly decreased in the last decade, printed stationery is another extension of your brand.

In the business of grabbing potential clients' attention, we have a narrow window to make the right first impression. You want to be present in people's minds long after you've left the room, and something kitsch in a cool, branded design will certainly help your case. If you can leave a stranger with a memorable business card, you are already building a connection with them. What they go on to say about meeting you is the brand you're building.

## Choose your wardrobe

"What has my wardrobe got to do with brand-building?" I can hear you asking. Well, hear me out. Remember I mentioned the meat dress and the snazzy glasses earlier? While those were extreme examples, the point stands that the way you dress can influence how you are perceived by your clients or audience.

If you ask a rock star to attend a brand collaboration meeting, they won't show up dressed like Barry from Accounts to fit in, and nor should you.

Just like every part of our brand building, what you wear is an expression of your personality and signature style, so follow your Feel and use it as a compass to show you the right direction for your personal wardrobe. You are what you wear, as they say (or if they don't say it, I'm saying it now).

# "You can't build a reputation on what you are going to do."

Henry Ford

Creativity for Sale

Pages
118—143

Chapter - no.5

# Amplify

Creativity for Sale

Amplify

Chapter - no.5

123. **This is only the beginning**
125. *Amplify your messaging*
127. Talking the talk
130. *Your digital shop window*
132. Who owns traffic?
134. *Amplify your connections*
138. The power of a newsletter
140. *To network or not to network?*
141. Do awards matter?
142. *If all of this sounds too much...*

Creativity for Sale

## Amplify

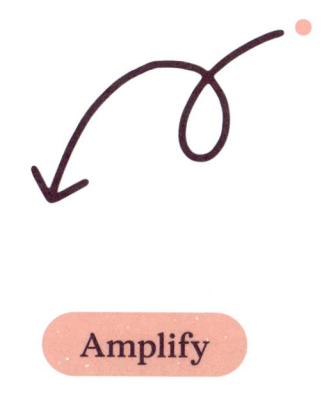

This chapter is all about putting your next set of foundational steps into action before getting out there and starting to run your creative business successfully. A newbie creative usually has two questions on their lips: "How do I get work?" and "How much does everyone charge?" In this chapter, we'll answer the first; and in the next chapter, Money, we'll answer the other.

### This is only the beginning

When you're first starting out, your work is two-fold: start your business and make sure you make the right people know that you exist. We'll be focusing on making fewer but stronger connections that are more valuable to your long-term success as they become deeper relationships, not collecting an army of followers (in case that wasn't clear from the previous chapter).

It might feel as though you have to spend more time on getting your name out there than getting stuck in with the actual creative work at first, but the good news is that you should only need to do this round once. Once you build a core roster of clients, the momentum amplifies from there.

Giant brands pump millions into ensuring we hear about and try their product through every available channel. It might take people weeks or longer to first notice the advertising, and secondly to buy the product (if they ever do). When you scale down the whole situation to consider your fledgling creative business, it seems as though you're pretty much invisible to the general public, and far from flying onto the radar of potential clients (also known as 'prospects'). But this is just the beginning, and it gets better from here.

If you are an employee of a creative business, your role contributes to the wider company as you're essentially a cog in a big machine. Other people look after promoting the business, working on lead generation, checking data from IP tracking software, analysing incoming website traffic, and so on before someone writes another 'thought leadership' article to appeal to a specific pool of prospective clients. But in a business of one, you are the cog, and it's down to you to move it forward, propping it up from all sides. You create the work. You build the business. You have to tell the right people about it. And then do the accounts. And the tax return.

The good news is that unlike the megabrands, you don't need to sell millions of tins of baked beans to keep everything going. You can focus on helping a much smaller number of clients by creating work that matters. And that's often much more fulfilling

## Amplify your messaging

In the last chapter, we've looked at how to build your portfolio with both physical and digital assets, and as much as you might like them to speak for you, the reality is that they can't always speak for themselves when it comes to landing clients. This is why your messaging is vital to your ongoing success.

As a business owner, you need confidence to succeed, and among many other things, confidence is born out of knowing that your messaging is right.

The Define section helped you establish the foundations of your business, your philosophy (i.e., what you stand for) and what you wish to achieve. These keep you personally on the right path, but you also need to translate these into words that make sense to your clients, customers, and other people so the world understands you and your path too. This is amplifying your messaging.

Your messaging can generally be tailored into three different lengths of text used for different situations depending on what information is required and what your desired outcome is.

**Version 1** – *Who are you, what is your title, and what do you do?*
**Version 2** – *Who are you, what is your title, what do you do, and what is your mission statement?*
**Version 3** – *Your personal brand statement and a short biography of who you are.*

In other words, your messaging is sometimes a casual, simple summary of who you are and what you do, but other times it's more formal, like a mission statement that tells the world what your company does, where it does it, why it exists, who its main customers are, and what it's aiming to achieve (the primary goal).

Personally, it took me a long time to narrow down what I wanted to say for each of these, as I wanted to tell everyone pretty much everything I was doing at any given time. Like I was a graphic designer who also did illustration, created apps and websites, directed the occasional music video, and made motion graphic pieces here and there. If I'd been more confident at the time, I would have just said "I'm a graphic designer", but I wanted to get across every nuance in case I was speaking to someone who needed those other skills — and in doing so, I probably came across as an unfocused, overzealous I-can-do-it-all.

The confidence to shorten it down comes with practice, and it's much easier to nail this when you've taken the time to focus on exactly what skills or products you're offering for exactly which group. Defining a small, niche group of customers will help with your messaging and targeting.

Just as it's tempting to over-label yourself with too many titles to appeal to a wider network of potential clients, it's equally tempting to big up the work you've done on projects and stretch the truth about your involvement, like saying you managed the whole project when you actually only did a tiny part of it. By all means make your work and process look hoppin', but be honest about what you do and offer. It makes everyone's life easier in the long term.

When you get your messaging right and things start to work out, it will likely feel great to finally see your efforts paying off, and this will increase your confidence, but beware that this doesn't slip into or get mistaken for arrogance. Sometimes, arrogance is a thinly veiled form of anxiousness, where the impostor is overshadowed by the boaster. Other times, the boaster isn't really boasting and is simply proud of what they've achieved. In most situations, it will be up to you to let people know what you stand for and how much you value your creative output, which might make people think you're arrogant, so think about what you say and how you say it. But, ultimately, be aware that making people take notice can come with both risks and rewards.

### Talking the talk

On the path of running your creative business, you'll need to acquire skills beyond those that directly affect your creative output, including your verbal communication. At first, it can feel like a drag having to get good at talking about your work and selling your brand of creativity, but always keep in mind that this path is the only one where you have control of your own destiny and success. And while talking might feel uncomfortable at first, the more work you put into expressing yourself and improving your speaking skills, the more benefits you'll see in the long term with customer conversions. We hope that our visual creations will do the talking and selling part on our behalf, but it's ultimately you who knows the most about your work and process, and therefore you're the best suited to be the most vocal about it.

For you, talking might be presenting your work to existing clients, sales calls with potential customers, or one-to-ones with collaborators; it might be hosting a podcast; or it might be doing talks or presentations within your industry. Either way, the principles of good communication are the same. To get good before you start talking, do your research and get prepared for what you're about to say. There's no better way than to learn from the good examples that you can find online. To improve your speaking skills, read out loud and test your presentation skills. Make it a habit and practise your speech daily for a while. Think about your breathing and composure. Our nerves often kick in when we're unprepared or fearing failure.

If necessary, hire a speaking coach for a few short lessons to correct any bad habits. You can watch TED talks to see what lands well and what doesn't, analyse Steve Jobs' presentations, and go to a few talks in your industry.

Make notes on how the person connects with and engages their audience, from their words to their tone, body language, clothing, and so on. Then examine how your findings can work with or against your own processes.

— What can you tell people that they can't already see?
— What does your process involve that makes your work succeed?
— What does your way of working involve that no one knows like you do?
— What unique insights or stories can you share to motivate people and compel action?
— What questions can you ask to unlock curiosity in your audience?

# Amplify

Public speaking can be an asset to building a personal brand, especially in a world that is hyper connected. These days, it's often banded about as the key feature to get your message out there. However, there are also plenty of people who got famous without doing a TED talk, and you can build a brand without needing to have a near panic attack or trying to deliver a speech without the worry of passing out or vomiting. If public speaking is something you've considered, always make sure you do it for the right reasons and motivation. It's easy to put your ego at the forefront instead of giving people valuable takeaways.

**Which type of person are you?**
— I'd like to do a talk about my work.
— I was asked to do a talk, and I think I'll do it but let me think about it.
— I can't think of anything worse than going on stage and speaking to a room full of strangers.

If the former, it can be a great journey amplifying yourself from talking to one person to presenting to a whole room and commanding their attention, but it takes time to grow into this level of confidence. It often helps to start small and work your way up the audience size, rather than diving straight onto a stage in front of hundreds of people. You might even start at home, reading books out loud to your cat. It's also the outcome of continuous practice and edits, so don't expect to be incredible the first time you get on stage, or even the fifth. Give it a dozen or so presentations before your nerves die down a little. Give it a few years and you'll be flying.

The process of getting speaking engagements is much the same as getting new clients. Very few speakers get approached directly by event organisers, and even some of the most established names have to get their pitch sent for consideration. Even though we've diverted from your client meeting onto the stage, the ability to speak about you and your work will unlock more than opportunities, and will make you more confident long term.

## Your digital shop window

When you're not able to talk in-person, your website often does that for you, and it acts as your elevator pitch without you being in the room. The challenge is that you have just a few seconds to make a first impression, but you're not physically there to explain any nuances that visitors might misunderstand. This is why it's an ongoing challenge to get your website messaging right to convert a casual passer-by into a potential customer there and then.

Your set of digital touchpoints, including your website, should clearly state who you are and what you do, and outline the sort of problems you can solve and which actions help you do so. You also need to make it clear where you're based, how to get in touch with you, and who you work with. Many prospective clients prefer to work with local people, while some are happy to forge a cross-continental link to get the right person for the job.

Most of your potential clients will want to pick up the phone (or do a Zoom video chat) to get an idea of what type of person is on the other end of the line. Even though it can take anywhere from a few days to a few months of conversations before a project starts, your prospects will want to cut down their shortlist as early as possible.

As mentioned in the previous chapter, your portfolio should be on your website, but remember that the words on your website (also known as 'copy') are just as important as the pretty images, if not more so, and you should always follow best practices when it comes to website design and experience as they exist for a reason.

To you and me, the creative process can seem obvious; you can look at a piece of creative work and tell how it was made with near perfect precision. However, a prospective client doesn't have that knowledge, so your case studies should document the process from start to finish in language that's easy to understand and contains the right search engine optimisation (SEO) keywords, which is a fancy way of saying 'what people are typing into Google'. Your website copy is for potential customers and the bots that index your website across all search engines, so SEO is vital.

I can't emphasise enough that your website can be the difference between scores of people contacting you in a week and none at all. I learned this the hard way when I re-launched my portfolio website with very minimal copy and a lot of project images.

For about three weeks, there was suspicious silence. No new work, no enquiries, nothing. I looked back at the design and added some simple copy in an 18pt font at the top of the site. It looked clunky, bold but it turned out to be necessary. It said who I was, what I did, and who I did it for: (this is my old statement)

*"Hello, I'm Radim Malinic, an award-winning graphic designer and illustrator based in London. I work with individuals and family businesses all the way to household brands and companies worldwide. Get in touch today and let's work together."*

My offering was broad back then, but it caught enough traffic to get frequent enquiries, so it did the trick.

## Who owns traffic?

As you may have noticed earlier, I'm not the biggest fan of putting too much focus on social media. Some people argue that social media is vital to gain traffic (i.e., people visiting your website and interacting with you as a brand), and I won't argue that social media can deliver traffic. However, a savvy business owner should understand how that traffic works, and who owns it.

Case in point: Back in 2013, there was a short video creation app called Vine. As it became increasingly popular, some users gained literally millions of followers and fans. But after 4 years and acquisition by a much bigger platform, Vine abruptly shut down and went offline as it failed to generate adequate revenues. Years of creative work that had been uploaded disappeared, and while many of the videos made it on to other platforms like YouTube, those with millions of followers were left empty-handed, so to speak. While Instagram and Tik Tok seem far too valuable to simply disappear right now, that might change one day; nobody expected MySpace to disappear, and yet it did.

The lesson is that no matter how many followers you gain, you won't have control over these platforms or the audience you gain from them. Plus, it's impractical and damn near impossible to pinpoint where your traffic is coming from on each specific post.

Still, many creative businesses would happily rely on traffic generated from social media, and pretty much every business uses such platforms as an extension of their brand's existence, an add-on in a very fragmented digital space. Brands go where people hang out, and they work hard to become part of a conversation. Smart brands, when they've got the attention of their audience, divert interest back towards their core offering on their website or in their physical store(s).

If social media is your main shop window, then you may struggle to offer the experience or information that will convert viewers into new business, and you are at the whim of such platforms' algorithms. By contrast, if you have a solid website, then you own your traffic and can analyse it far better. Having an online presence that's all yours, and not subject to the whims of other corporations, helps you stay in control.

Then, if you work on your search engine visibility, your traffic will grow organically over time. If you spend time digging deeper into the SEO of your website, you'll have a huge head-start over your creative peers as these methods are almost criminally overlooked by many. If you don't want to learn SEO yourself, then hire a specialist to run monthly reports with suggestions.

A word of warning: SEO is not an overnight process, and it takes time to build your visibility, often almost six months to a year to get your desired results. If you want to be visible right from the start, then the answer might be Pay Per Click (PPC) advertising, which can turbo-charge your traffic. Both cost money, but the former will likely spread your budget out over longer. Either way, track your analytics, i.e., how many people are visiting your site, where they're based, and other vital information. Though remember that you'll keep them on your site with compelling copy and useful insights, not just a bunch of keywords.

### Amplify your connections

As I said earlier, the best way to build your clientele or customer base is to form real connections with those you work with and for. Your long-term success depends on the quality of your work, of course, but also on the quality of your connections and relationships with your customers and clients, and your reputation, which travels fast. This means you shouldn't rush to work with everyone right away for the wrong reasons.

New connections can come your way in the form of new client enquiries, recommendations, or personal introductions, but either way, you need to grow them into meaningful connections. A meaningful connection is one where you both grow your respective businesses in tandem through the project; it's not a one-way street or a simple transaction like buying orange juice at the self-checkout. If you can land ongoing collaborations rather than one-off commissions, you will get to explore your creativity further, build on your successes, and learn from your mistakes.

So, where do you find these people to start forming connections? Always start by connecting with the people you already know, and don't be afraid to ask for an introduction if someone you know knows someone who you want to know.

Then move on to the people you definitely don't know but want to know. Some people and businesses add hundreds of people on LinkedIn and shotgun the same generic message to them. But if you were to send thousands of generic dating app messages, you'd likely be met with silence and tumbleweed, right? It's the same with running a creative business. Shooting wide can feel tempting, and it's certainly simple, but it's not the key to success. It's impersonal and pointless.

I don't think I should have to say this, but I'm going to say it anyway: don't send out hundreds of automated pre-scripted emails or LinkedIn messages, essentially 'cold calling' potential clients. You no doubt receive daily emails and messages from every man and his dog who is keen to pitch their services, and do you feel treasured and special? No. It's blatantly obvious that the conversation isn't tailored to you personally, but the process of selling or marketing. And that is fine; if it didn't work for them at some point, they wouldn't do it. But this is not the way to build genuine connections; it's far more effective to personalise your messages for individuals.

To clarify, I'm not saying never email someone you don't know. I'm saying don't send the same generic message to hundreds of people as they will see through it. Pick a select group of people you genuinely want to connect with, then send something that's tailored to them. Also understand that trying to land clients doesn't always mean shouting about what you do; sometimes it means shouting about what they do. If a client you'd love to work with launches a new product, take the chance to compliment them on it. They'll likely be in a good mood and excited about their latest endeavour, so make the most of this and introduce yourself. Some brands look out for creative collaborators, so it's a good opportunity to get on their radar.

This has worked for me many times. Instead of pitching my services to someone who has no idea who I am, I express my feelings and admiration about the work they do. They're usually genuinely engaged and interested, and a compliment can go a long way in building a connection for later.

Note: There's a key difference in cold emailing vs cold DMing on social media. For emails, the golden number to get a reply is six messages spread out across a few days and weeks. For DMs, six unsolicited might make you look a bit desperate. Either way, the key is having the right tone: be personal, be curious, and be specific, with a clear call to action for them to make.

To truly amplify your work is to continually generate interest in what you do. But this starts with you, and it's vital that you are creating momentum, continually moving forwards. Keeping up momentum can feel challenging, and quieter times naturally make everyone panic that no work is coming in, but resist the temptation to send dozens of panic emails hoping that someone will magically reply within a few minutes with a life-changing piece of work. Desperation at such times is inevitable, but it can be avoided with proactive work.

One proven trick is to send at least one email a day to someone in your network. This builds momentum and means you stay on people's radar. You can assign them into groups according to their importance, like clients or collaborators > potential clients and brands > industry contacts, or like-minded creatives. Your email might be for the purposes of generating interest in your work, keeping in touch with previous clients, sending a compliment to a podcast host, or sending a personalised work update. Each only takes a few minutes to write and send.

This method has worked for me for years, and I still send an email a day. It gives the impression that there's a constant buzz going on, even when I'm not on the lookout for new projects or collaborations. By sending an email each day on an ongoing basis, there's no heightened sense of expectation or needing someone to reply. You just tell the world you exist and that your business is healthy, and who knows where that will take you.

Note: When it comes to emailing, only write an email when you know exactly what you want to say. Then reread it, shorten it, and shorten it some more. Think about it from the perspective of the recipient: Does it make sense? What do you want from it? Impulsive gibberish may only take a few seconds to write, but it might spend a lifetime sitting in an inbox unread.

I once told a client that I would be charging him for reading his emails as they were endless verbal meanders that didn't achieve any purpose. After chomping through the sludge of his thoughts, I'd still have to pick up the phone and work out what on earth I was meant to be doing. So, my top tip is to get it all down in five sentences, no more, and set out the action you want the person to do next, which means they will need to reply. It might feel a bit pushy or even a bit unnatural to do, but it's easier for both you and the client, and it saves a lot of time and hassle.

## The power of a newsletter

Another way to amplify your connections and engagement is through email marketing. You might think this sounds a little old school compared to the immediacy of social media, but viral trends come and go while email stands firm and is one of the single most effective ways of getting your voice out there. While you could share your passions through a YouTube channel, podcast, or blog, consider the vast amount of content that is created by each of these methods every day, which you're competing against to get attention.

If you want people to pay attention to you and your work, and you want to nurture individual connections, then build up your email list and look after it. Think about email marketing as a way to add value to your subscribers. Your ultimate goal might be to make a sale or get commissioned, or make money, but your main aim should be establishing a line of communication that adds value for them first.

As you nail down what you do and what you stand for, and as you build on your magic formula, you'll develop a singular voice in your industry, and this is what adds value. Those who stand out are the ones who are passionate about their subject, really understand it in depth, and are willing to share their knowledge. It's another way of making meaningful connections with those who are aligned with your philosophies and ideas.

To capture email addresses, add an email sign-up feature to your website. This is often featured in the website footer design to make it visible without being too overwhelming or desperate.

This is often the immediate pop-up window asking you to sign up to a website you haven't even seen yet.

To give people a good reason to sign up for your emails, the first step is to create a 'lead magnet', which is a free piece of content that is of value. For example, '10 ways to master your creative process!' that can be downloaded or read via a welcome email to your mailing list. Of course, some people will inevitably only come for the freebie and then unsubscribe from your future emails, but email marketing retention rates are high overall, so it's always worth trying.

In the following emails, introduce yourself and your work, and make sure you add value without pampering your ego. You might have a finite pool of process insights to share, but there's an infinite world of resources and insights out there, so don't worry that you'll run out of things to say. A regular info-mail with valuable content, no industry jargon, and low sales-pushing yields great results in the long term, though if you're planning to sell, then don't push this until at least the fourth email or people will quickly start hitting 'unsubscribe'.

As with my other knocks and bruises, of course, I learned this the hard way. I bought a list of emails, put together a newsletter that said "Look at MEEEEEE! This is my work!", sent the campaign out, and — surprise, surprise — got no response. Just think: how many emails, display adverts, social media adverts, website pop-ups, and input forms did you ignore or close today alone? Likely a countless amount. My emails were another tiny spec of noise in someone's daily mix of incoming traffic.

Even in the rare instance that you interact with an advert

and consider buying, it might take you a while to decide whether you're going to buy the product or service. The higher the price, the longer the time it takes to pull the trigger. If your creative services are priced on the lower side, there might be more interest and more traffic as a lower price tag bears less risk for the client and is more likely to convert into a project. And conversely, if you command higher prices, you convert fewer prospects into clients as the ratio decreases with the percentage. But either way, the likelihood of a sale increases when people know you and your brand, and connection-building takes time.

It's very easy to get emotionally invested in expecting quick results for every effort you make. But just like the people behind every advert you didn't click on today knows, it takes time before they will see a return from their actions. The key is to form real connections, then let those people know that your brand of creativity exists, what it stands for, and where to find it. Once they are ready, you'll see a return on all the energy you've put into it.

A word of warning: As with any activity that isn't primarily 'what you do'. Just like social media, this is an add-on, so make sure this content generation doesn't side-track you from your main business. These activities can become time thieves until you learn to produce them quickly or you outsource or automate them.

### To network or not to network?

Of course, online isn't the only way to form connections, and many businesspeople swear by networking. While networking events certainly work for some people, my personal feeling is that they can be a waste of time. I've given them a shot so many times and yet always come away confused about what just happened.

Still, some creatives find them effective to a certain extent, so if you want to give networking a go, you have two options. Either you can approach it as a place to find and form genuine connections that you might convert over the long term, or you can have your elevator pitch at the ready, take a handful of your snazzy business cards, and make the most of any encounters with prospective clients. The latter might lead you to look 'salesy', but it's also better than turning up unprepared.

A helpful tip: Many networking hopefuls are nervous about being in an environment that's outside their comfort zone, so aim for more curated events that are specifically targeted to your industry or audience, and if you're really nervous, do some power-posing before going into the room (preferably where nobody can see you), or look at the delegates list in advance, connect with a few people on LinkedIn, and agree to meet them in person at the event. If that sounds like too much effort, hang around outside the door to the event and say hi to the first person who arrives after you, then you can walk in together.

## Do awards matter?

Many neighbourhood restaurants in the UK have walls groaning with a myriad of awards declaring their successes from years or even decades ago. But for the vast majority of customers, these certificates are near meaningless as we've no idea what they were awarded for. And often, we don't care as it's the food that keeps us coming back, not the awards.

Creative awards are arguably often similar. Aiming for prestigious awards right out the gate is an encouraging sign that you take your business seriously, but it can be equally disheartening to see the big guns win all of the top accolades. Though many are judged according to a strict set of criteria, creativity-based awards can also seem subjective and ultimately subject to the particular tastes of whoever is judging that category. As such, awards can be an emotional rollercoaster. Entering them can also take up a lot of your time, which can be a distraction.

The plus side of entering awards is that if you win, you have a legit reason to call yourself an award-winning creative, and the feeling of someone, somewhere, recognising your work is fantastic. Ultimately, being able to label yourself as 'award-winning' can help your reputation, but just like an award-winning restaurant, it doesn't matter whether and what you've won to many people. To them, it only matters if you can deliver the work well, every single time. Your reputation doesn't come printed and framed on the wall, after all.

### If all of this sounds too much...

You've made it to the end of this chapter. How do you feel about all of the work that needs doing? Not everyone will see this set of actions as something they want to do personally, and there's nothing wrong with that. There are plenty of options available to help you with all of this. Some creatives have agents or virtual assistants to amplify their message and awareness. Remember to seek assistance or guidance before these points become easier.

"85% of your financial success is due to your personality and ability to communicate, negotiate, and lead. Shockingly, only 15% is due to technical knowledge."

Carnegie Institute of Technology

Creativity for Sale

Pages

# 144—169

# Chapter - no.6
# Money

Creativity for Sale

Money

Chapter - no.6

**149.** Calculate your baseline

**151.** *Put a value on your creativity*

**157.** What is your value?

**159.** *The value of long-term clients*

**160.** The value of long-term work

**162.** *When is it not worth it?*

**163.** How to get paid

**166.** *How to chase non-payments*

Creativity for Sale

## Money

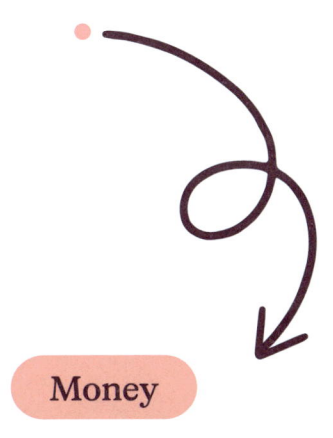

If the first 'billion dollar' business question is 'Where do I get clients?', then a very close second is 'What do I charge?' To answer that question, many people ask about what everyone else charges, and likely wonder why so few people talk openly about what they earn. That's why this chapter discusses the topic of money, and in an open and transparent way.

### Calculate your baseline

A creative business is considerably cheaper to get off the ground than many other sectors. You don't need a car or a van, expensive machinery, huge premises, supply materials, or a warehouse full of stock. And while a reasonably powerful laptop can be more expensive than a second-hand Ford Fiesta, it's not out of reach like it was a few decades ago.

To find out your basic survival budget as a one-person creative business, add up the following (some won't be relevant of course, and other things might need to be added):

**Business expenses:**
— Hardware + Software
— Business insurance
— Studio space rental + Office supplies + Overheads
— Cost of commute
— Bank or transaction fees
— Tax

**Personal expenses:**
— Travel + Food + Rent/mortgage
— Mobile phone bill + Internet connection
— Clothing + Social life budget
— Gym membership

Knowing your costs should serve as the baseline from which you start building your price. In employed jobs, your desired salary is often based on years in work, experience, job, and location. In a small creative business, the flow of incoming work and steadiness of progress is usually far more unpredictable. No two projects will be the same, and they won't have the same budget or take the same amount of time to complete.

However, knowing your costs will guide you because you'll know how much you need to earn to survive, and from there you can work out how much you'd need to thrive.

The aim here is to spend more hours working on your own business rather than working for someone else's.

## Put a value on your creativity

Once you know how much you need to make, then you can start costing your work. With pricing, it's about balancing the time it takes to do the work with the value of the work, and there are different ways to calculate this cost. Most people start out with their own preferred method of calculating costs, but as they start taking on new clients, they might switch things up and move to other methods. And, of course, each method has its pros and cons.

A freshly set up creative business is more likely to bill by time (per hour or per day), so at least at the start, understanding how much time it takes to produce creative work is usually the main driver of how it's priced. However, once you've established your brand of creativity and defined your offering clearly, then the value of the project might dictate the overall cost, though it might take a few years to get from the former to the latter.

**Cost per hour** - In my opinion, charging by the hour is the messiest way to quantify the cost of creativity. An hour in the life of a creative can feel like a second since a piece of work can contain so many unknowns and lead to multiple explorations. So, if you bill by the hour, the key is to add up the number of hours needed for the work and add in an extra few (or more than a few) as a buffer for any possibilities and issues.

One of the positives of charging per hour is the freedom to juggle different projects and work when based on your availability without too many constraints. However, a downside is that clients often like to negotiate on the rate, especially if the project is open-ended, and they might feel that it's easier to find someone who they won't have to pay as much, particularly if they have a cap on their monthly spending. The benefits of working in a free-flowing way can also be outweighed by having less financial stability.

Charging per hour also involves having tracking software to help you calculate a final amount that is reflective of the actual hours spent. Quite a few freelancers run a clock and charge an amount in increments of an hour. For example, changing a word on a page might take 15 minutes, so does it really need an hourly charge? This should be decided by the creative and made clear to the client, who might be more inclined to run the clock instead of an hour block.

**Cost per day -** This option is more streamlined, although the actual meaning or expectation of day rates can often be confusing.

The first interpretation is that a creative supplier is booked for a full day of work, i.e., eight hours of the day. Then, companies hire people for their specific skill set for a number of days per week or month. The upside is that if there's any hold ups, you're still being paid even though the work is at a stand-still. And if you get your work done in a fraction of the time, you're still paid the full day rate. The downside is that the deliverables, milestones, and expectations need to be very clear to both parties beforehand.

The second interpretation is bulk-buying hours in advance. A day rate could be a guarantee of a block of eight hours that should cover the time to produce the right outcome. The work can be produced across the number of days in small increments as and when the project requires, just like charging by the hour. But instead of the client haggling over the hours, they're committed to a chunk of time in advance.

The positive here is the knowledge that you have a set amount of time covered in advance, and it's also the case that companies paying day rates are often higher ticket clients, meaning there might be a better sense of financial security and planning. But before you accept a day rate, make sure it's clear what the expectations are as you don't want any surprises later. The prospect of having a set income might be tempting, but you might lose some of your freedom to juggle projects or assist more clients at the same time.

**A retainer -** This is another form of 'bulk buying' time. But instead of blocking out hours per day or days per week/month, there is an hourly allowance per month. The retainer guarantees a set monthly figure against a set of deliverables. The benefit of this method is an ongoing month-to-month commitment from the client.

In all of these time-based methods, the deliverables need to be clearly defined, as well as the time it should take to complete them. If you exceed the agreed hours or days and present a higher bill without any prior explanation or warning, it can make for an interesting conversation. When extra time is needed, put your hand up and make it clear why.

**Project rate -** This is when the price may be based on the value of the project rather than the time required to do the work. For example, a project rate might be based on the market cost and the level of skills, knowledge, and experience that goes into making the idea a reality. Or it might be based on the number of days and people required for these more intricate and varied services. Though, calculating a project rate based on the average time it takes you to produce such work is tricky if you're new, and this is another reason why new creatives don't tend to price this way. Perhaps the best way to think of a project rate is time bulk buying plus an added premium, but it's always worth factoring in the scope of deliverables, which should be laid out in a project brief, specification, or 'statement of work'. Some creatives are near militant in the price quoted for the project specification, so if they agree X, then they are delivering X and nothing else. This makes a lot of sense from an admin perspective, but the unpredictability of creative work can make X become Y pretty quickly. Then, do you start negotiating again or just do Y? The list of deliverables can easily change, and creative projects generally require being adaptable and fluid in response to changing requirements.

I believe there are many positives to charging a one-off price per project. The main benefit is that both parties have full knowledge of the overall cost at the beginning of the engagement, and there should be no reason to haggle over small details or have to recalculate if the client adds a few extra deliverables to the list. It can make you seem more confident in negotiations when you have a clear cost for your work, rather than getting out the calculator and trying to pin the client down to a specific number of hours.

**Equity** - The final pricing option is equity, which essentially means getting a share of a company. In other words, not getting paid in money right now, but in shares, so potentially more money in the future.

When a prospective client offers you a hefty part of their

company rather than payment, it's often a giveaway that they are not a trading company yet. So, you're betting on the future of a company where you don't control its operations or business strategy. Many new start-ups are keen to get their launch across the line with next to no money, so they shop around for people who are willing to work for free, meaning the offer of equity could be a red flag.

The other obvious downside is that you won't get paid for the work yet, or even for a long time. Having a stake in a company that earns zero is still, well, zero. Even if the company starts making money, equity isn't liquid cash available when you need it. It comes to fruition only when the company gets sold. This could ultimately be a profitable strategy, but it's not a solution to get your mortgage paid next month.

On the contrary, there are many success stories of creative services being traded for shares in companies leading to very handsome profits. You might also form a business connection that is valuable when the company is trading and appreciates what you did for them in the early days.

To make the equity work, you will have to negotiate the right terms and conditions, which takes longer than a napkin sketch at your first meeting. So, don't get seduced by a convincing sales pitch, and do your research into the company. Ask your accountant for further tax advice if this situation comes up.

**The budget shootout -** Some freelancers approach the issue of pricing like a shootout — they keep their weapon in their pocket and wait to see who draws first. In other words, they ask the client what their budget is before sharing their cost. This might be because they want to see the most the client will offer, or because they haven't taken the time to define their offering and calculate a cost.

Either way, this is a risky move. The client will always have a figure in mind that they can spend, but they generally don't want to disclose it in case they can make a saving. They'd rather the creative play their hand first so they can see what they've got. However, the creative doesn't want to in case they quote too low and the client has a bigger budget. This is a spectacular showcase of blink first and you've lost. This is up there with the best of the worst negotiating tactics, and is a source of very funny memes too.

**Working for free -** Many creatives, especially those first starting out, have a 'dream' client list, usually filled with global household name brands. Such brands are aware of their shiny status, and some try to exploit this by offering creative talent laughably small fees, or no fee at all.

Some consider the opportunity, shake their head in disbelief at how ridiculous it is, then agree to do the work anyway because the brand's power is seductive. From my first-hand experience, these projects often go excellently badly, and the opportunity turns into a spectacular nightmare. But you can learn a lot from the experience. Heavily discounted or free work is often best pursued for an opportunity to learn, explore new media, help a good cause, or be part of something that has the potential to grow. The work shouldn't feel pressured or restrictive, the collaboration should be inclusive, and both sides should be working towards the same goal. If this doesn't add up, don't dance. Pass.

Money

## What is your value?

A piece of art is only worth as much as someone is willing to pay for it. But this doesn't just apply to art; it applies to anything in life where the price changes according to scarcity, exclusivity, or perceptions about its value, and there's a lot of value in solutions and those who can provide them.

When it comes to business, those solutions might be in the form of business plans or audits, useability reports, brand strategies, or marketing blueprints. Business problems that need solving often bubble under the surface for a while until someone makes a plan of action to solve them. Then, the need for a solution is often rational, practical, and pragmatic.

Many years ago, I heard about a freelance developer who went to see a potential client, in person like it was the norm some years ago. He sat in the waiting room, only to see a few other people exit the 'war room' of a coding conundrum. After the greetings and handshake, the conversation went swiftly onto the project and its required solution.

Once the freelancer had heard the full score, he took a breath and exhaled a relieved sigh. "The solution is pretty straightforward and will only take a few hours to fix." The room fell silent, and the clients' faces revealed a look of surprise. "It will only cost £500 to fix." One of the team replied, "Ha, that's interesting. We just had an agency here that told us it will take a month and £15,000 in project fees."

The freelancer didn't win the project, and we can learn from this story. First, you will generally have no idea who you're competing against when pitching for a project, unlike the freelancer watching the war room door, so don't try to base your rates on what you think others are charging, especially as your pricing might look a lot different to your competitors' if you don't have to factor in the costs of running a whole agency and hiring employees. Second, make sure you listen closely and understand exactly what the client requires so you don't accidentally underestimate or overestimate your costs. Third, it's very tempting to 'big up' the scope of a solution to possible clients to charge a higher cost, but they might see through the charade.

Ultimately, the key is to propose an appropriate and honest figure that is right for the problem and its solution, and your own experience level and knowledge. Regardless of the various market considerations and comparable industries, the key in every cost is whether the client can pay and whether you can deliver what they need, which in essence is about trust and reliability.

— Is it clear what you offer and how you'll solve the problem?
— Are you honest with your prospects or do you sprinkle a little BS on top to win the work?
— Can you actually deliver what the client is asking for?
— Are you too keen to close the deal without fully understanding the brief?

There will always be a difference in the price submitted from various creatives in the mix. Sometimes, the decision on who to choose isn't judged on the total estimated figure but how the person or business proposes to solve the problem. This means detailing the process, giving a full scope of the action, and telling the client the estimated length of time it will take. In this way, they will understand that bigger projects require additional resources, with extra costs attached.

## The value of long-term clients

Some of my clients have been with me for more than a decade, and others even longer. There's something so valuable in continuous collaboration that pushes both sides to keep producing good work, grow both businesses, and achieve things we didn't even know were possible when we started out.

At the start of your journey, you don't have a name for yourself, and so being realistic, clients aren't likely to put forward vast sums of money for results they can't be sure they'll get.

For that reason, which I now truly understand, only 1 in 20 of the projects I proposed a cost for were actually agreed for that amount. The other 19 had a decent budget for their project, which at the time felt a bit short based on the true market value and what I could provide for what they needed, but I went with it anyway. In such situations, you can make one of two decisions: either you can negotiate some more or you size up the long-term value of the client and go with that rationale. I preferred the latter option.

When you put the focus on finance over creativity, it sets a tone that will always be focused on budget constraints instead of creative solutions. I'm not saying you shouldn't discuss money, because you have to, of course. I am saying that discussing the creative solution should come first, and cost negotiations shouldn't become a big thing. Plus, if you get the client on board with your solution and vision for them, they are more likely to pay whatever you're proposing.

As most of us know, when Amazon first started out, it was an online bookseller and in no way a ground-breaking business model. It wasn't a profitable business either, not at the beginning. Now, you and I both know that Amazon is one of the most valuable and profitable companies in the world. They still sell books, and you might be surprised to know that they still sell them at a loss. Why do they do this? Because they see value in keeping customers in the long term. It doesn't matter if the customer acquisition happens on a low-ticket item that doesn't make them a quick profit. It's about how much they could be spending in the future across many available products. This is what makes Amazon the biggest product search engine in the world, not Google. It's the place where people search for new products or solutions and are only one click away from making a purchase.

In the business of creativity, you can spend far too much time negotiating the right cost and lose an opportunity to retain a long-term client who will grow into a high-ticket buyer. Sometimes, you might have to kiss a few frogs in this process, but the long-term thinking pays off if you have the right business mindset, like Amazon, and the drive to grow and explore future opportunities.

## The value of long-term work

Conversely, there are situations where the client is looking for a one-off project, with a defined start and finish, and they won't need any further services from you as the problem is solved. On these occasions, I don't want you to think like Jeff 'the oddly shaped rocket owner' Bezos, but like a builder.

Many years ago, my wife and I wanted to renovate our house. We had our vision, ideas, dreams, and an earmarked budget. It was our very first 'building' project and therefore our thinking was unclouded by previous knowledge. We were spurred on by 'the fuel', and we wanted to build a grand design. At the start, such lofty visions are best approached without knowing how much they will actually cost, but at some point, someone has to put a price on your dream. So, we appointed an architect and explored the options of how best to optimise our dwelling for the future. However, as soon as things got exciting when we could see what our house might look like, we also faced reality head on when a few builders quoted us for the work.

The five quotes varied significantly, but we picked the one who was the most expensive and the most trustworthy. I thought my self-certified negotiating skills would come to play perfectly, except they didn't. The quote was final and there was no negotiation. "Could we do something about the numbers?" I asked. The answer was a firm no. The bricks cost money. The other materials cost money. The work was going to take six months.

It cost a lot, but we agreed on the basis that we understood the long-term value of the work — a beautiful, secure, and well-renovated house. We could have spent less, and we could have ended up with a nightmare being built instead of a dream.

In a creative business, you can add up each individual element in the equation and produce a final cost, which is simply that: the project cost. When the prospect sees the itemised list of deliverables and actions to achieve it, they will get a full picture of the whole project. A few potential clients will want to lower the price, but this is where you should know your worth and value. Sure, the client may have underestimated how much it would cost them, just like we did. But it doesn't mean they don't need to get the work done. An authoritative voice and approach can sway the work in your favour here, and super clear communication is key.

Whilst some days, you can shave off a few numbers to build a long-term client relationship, other days, you will need to stand your ground and build the house for what it should cost.

## When is it not worth it?

When a sizeable financial opportunity is presented to a creative for the first time, it's not often that they can fully concentrate on what's being asked of them. "Holy shit, how much did you say?!" is something they wouldn't say out loud for fear of looking inexperienced, but inside, they're wracking their brain about how to make it work and where to start. The reality is, projects can be agreed even without the freelancer having the necessary skills and knowledge, let alone experience.

I've done this. I agreed to take on work that I wasn't the right person for. I thought I needed the cash and wanted to do the work. Would I have taken the job if it had been priced at a much lower rate? I was a rookie idiot once upon a time, so maybe I would, but being offered a high price made me change my heart and ignore my mind. Many years later, I made the same mistake only in reverse when commissioning creative work. The inevitable car crash happened when I came across people who replicated my naive escapades from the early years. Even though I could spot the warning signs right from the start, I still was led to believe they were the right people to do the work, only to look for contingency solutions when the first choice didn't work out.

I don't believe that creative people are inherently greedy, and if they were, I'm sure they wouldn't bother choosing a career in this industry. However, any insecurities about the health of our finances and the predictable unpredictability of incoming work can make the best of us accept work that we should have left well alone. We've all been guilty of taking on work that's really meant for somebody else, and it takes a long time to become confident enough to pass on what doesn't feel right, even if it's temptingly well-paid.

### How to get paid

Now for some quick tips on getting paid, because payment can turn into a nightmare. Please note that you can download email template scripts for some of these actions via the bonus content link at the back of the book.

**Be clear with your payment terms** - Usually, invoices are paid within 30 days of the invoice date as standard, though some companies set their own terms to pay their suppliers later, such as 45 days or even up to 60 days. This is often clearly stated in the contract. State your terms on your contract. Your clients might be a little confused if you start chasing your payment within your own set payment terms that weren't mentioned in negotiations.

It's easy to be keen to get paid within a much shorter amount of time, but it needs to be flagged up. Otherwise, it looks very awkward.

**Don't send your invoices too early -** You've finished the work and supplied the files. Before the client can even approve the delivery, an invoice for the work slams into their inbox. It makes you look efficient, sure, but it can also be in bad taste. Get the work approved and then invoice.

**But... a regular client won't mind an early invoice -** There's an exception here. With clients that you know and have a proven track record with, you can sometimes invoice early. For example, if you know that the work will take a month to create and the same time to get the invoice paid, you can issue the invoice at the beginning of the project. Just check with them first.

**Half upfront, the rest on completion -** This is a common practice across many industries and can often work in your favour. Some clients want to secure creative services by making a part payment, often half of the project fee upfront before the work has begun. The second half is due either on supply of the work or within 30 days of that. Either way, the contract should state when the final amount is payable.

**Size doesn't always add up** - Smaller client projects are tend to be easier to get started, but often take longer to get paid. Bigger work can takes endless days and weeks to start but these payments can often be credited 'next day'. It can also feel like a second job to keep track of payments, contacts, and outstanding balances, but with thoughtful communication it's not too much drama.

**How to get protected** - You also need to make sure you're legally covered for any inevitable challenges. The following documents and policies can help you 'hope for the best, prepare for the worst', as the saying goes:

**Statement of work (SOW)** - This document provides a list of project requirements. It defines the scope of work with a list of the deliverables and estimated timelines, where the work takes place, and any other information that provides clarity for both parties. Usually, the client creates this, but make sure it's in place.

**Contract** - This two-way document incorporates the statement of work, with clear conditions on the project cost, how the work is agreed and delivered, and more. Some creatives won't get up in the morning until a contract is signed. Then some creatives, like me, don't have a contract for the first fifteen years of trading. Ultimately, I learned that especially for higher ticket projects, contracts make all the difference as clients stop having silly ideas about delayed payments. The client or the freelancer might have their own contract, and whoever's you choose, make sure you're both happy with it.

**Business insurance** - Again, some freelancers never bother to get insured, while others have insurance from day one. Insurance is one of those things that you don't think you need until you need it. Business losses if something goes wrong can be huge, so for the sake of a few hundred quid, get your insurance in place and save the heartache later if the worst happens. There are plenty of companies and brokers who can advise on what types you need, from public liability to professional indemnity.

With indemnity insurance, if you make a mistake, deliver a project late, or deliver it with such inferior quality that it negatively affects the client's trading, they might consider starting legal action against you to recover the loss of trading revenue. This could feel like the end of the world unless you've got this type of insurance. It gets you out of a hole.

## How to chase non-payments

Even with the most robust fail safes in place, sometimes a client won't pay on time. These circumstances sometimes come about when a verbal agreement, rather than a written contract, has been made, like when the project's communication moves faster than the admin side of things.

The majority of non-payments are due to simple reasons and are rarely malicious or intentional, and unless you're unluckily dealing with a hustler who ghosted you, there's every chance that you'll eventually get paid.

So, here are some tips on late payment:

**Late payment insurance -** As the name suggests, you can purchase insurance that covers you when your invoice funds aren't forthcoming. But this insurance can be misleading as there's no magic pot of money that will provide you with full payment if your client doesn't pay, or that your insurer will go after your debtor. Instead, it often provides legal services that advise you how to pursue the money owed.

**Pursuing debt -** When a payment is outstanding, the longer it takes for the non-payee to respond with a constructive response, the more likely the non-paid one is to feel resentful and annoyed. Communication is often the key to resolving this situation peacefully. If you don't hear back from the debtor, send a few neutrally toned email reminders. Some small companies even set up a fictional character and email address to make it look to debtors like they've got an accounts receivable department, and it turns out this works really well. And as mentioned earlier, always ask for a reply in an email — this time to get the status update and payment date.

**How to escalate -** If your invoice is unpaid beyond 60 days, you can up the tone of the language and stipulate what might happen in the case of non-payment. At this stage, the suggestion of getting a debt collection agent involved can produce almost instant results. Bigger companies don't want legal action against them. You can find email scripts in the bonus content section.

**When that doesn't work -** If they still don't pay, the next step is to appoint a debt collection agency to act on your behalf. If the issue gets this far, it's best to transfer the work over to the agent and let them do their thing, which does not mean kicking down someone's door or threatening them. However, these professionals work on commission, and they make sure they get the job done. They establish contact with the debtor and ensure there's no dispute over the work delivery or costs.

Then they negotiate a favourable outcome, which might be a staggered payment plan or full sum received.

Just make sure you understand the terms and conditions of the recovery agent, as you don't want any hidden fees to surprise you at any point.

**Legal action and costs** - A minority of debtors still may not pay what they owe, even if they agree to instalments or full payment. Debt recovery agents can help you escalate the matter further i.e., pursuing legal action in court. At this stage, there are upfront costs for the legal paperwork and court fees, which could make an unpaid invoice start to feel like a burden, especially as you have to part with further funds just to get paid for the work you've already done. To add further insult to injury, even a court judgement in your favour doesn't guarantee the debtor will pay, and the next level of escalation is paying a bailiff to knock on their door and seize their assets to the value of the total sum. As you can imagine, this is messy and complicated, and something best avoided.

And with that, let's get back to talking about what I prefer to talk about: creativity.

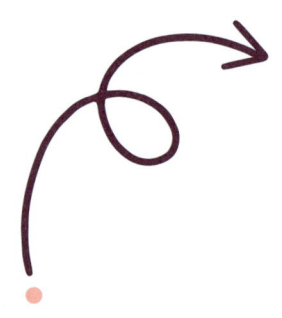

> "All you need is the plan, the road map, and the courage to press on to your destination."

Earl Nightingale

Creativity for Sale

Pages
# 170–191

Chapter - no.7

# Clients

Creativity for Sale

## Chapter - no.7

**175.** *Working for, or with, others*
**176.** Big or small fish?
**178.** *Managing emotions*
**179.** Keeping your eyes open
**180.** *Dealing with enquiries*
**187.** Doing the work

Creativity for Sale

## Working for, or with, others

    The nature of working with and for others can open up a lot of new horizons, experiences, and opportunities. Indeed, we can invent our own dream future by building our own brand of creativity. When something is made out of nothing, it can produce the most amazing feeling of accomplishment. However, getting creative work right for other people is a mastery in its own right. When more than one person is involved in the process, it can open up added opinions, speculations, and suggestions based on previous experiences, or the lack thereof.

    When you collaborate, you set the stage for that sometimes-dreaded other 'C word': *compromise*. When you're younger, compromise can feel like selling out or lowering your ambitions. In reality, compromise is about growth; it shows you new ways to learn and accept that input from others can create the best outcome. To compromise is to tune in to the right questions to produce the best answers. Compromise comes in many disguises

— and whether you redefine, adapt, absorb, learn, change, or improve something, it's an essential part of providing creative services and solutions.

Working for or with others comes with other challenges like communication (yes, there's a lot of C words here). Being able to work with others means you have to understand others and make them understand you, and this means you have to be accountable for how you communicate with people and play an active role.

Naturally, working with people isn't always easy or smooth, the same way as any human interaction. People have off days. We all make mistakes. It's all part of the process. At times, things will feel frustrating, but every collaboration, no matter how challenging, offers valuable lessons in understanding people.

## Big or small fish?

When it comes to choosing your clients, does size matter? A small operation with small clients can be a steady business, and a happy one too. On the flip side, another small business may be hell-bound on hyper growth, landing the biggest name clients and projects. Both, as you might expect, have their pros and cons.

The internet is flooded with memes about the ease of getting paid larger sums by big-ticket clients, which can make some creatives think it's far easier to work with bigger clients on bigger projects. The truth is that it's never that easy and it's not always that hard.

If you want to handle projects 20x the size, they might come with 20x the budget, but you will need 20x your operations and capability. No magic fairy drops tens of thousands of £$€ in budget without wanting a return on every single coin. To state the obvious, bigger work comes with bigger rewards and even bigger headaches. There's also no guarantee that higher value ticket clients' work will be more fun or engaging than work that is a fraction in size. Bigger corporations are often tangled in red tape where an invoice can get lost in complicated procurement software before it gets processed, approved, and paid.

By contrast, smaller projects can offer more freedom and satisfaction, as what you're making matters, and there's less risk so it won't, or shouldn't, keep you awake at night. Having an army of 'smaller clients' makes for a granular business as you finish the work or lose a client and the bag is still full. A bit like a bag of skittles. But you'll probably need a lot of these to pay your bills, and you have to factor in the time taken to manage multiple clients, as each one will require communication. Plus, a handful of one-off projects will require more regular time for retention in the case of any losses than a handful of long-term clients, so the type of project matters too. Smaller clients might have too much on their plate and lose their concentration on your project or struggle to pay your invoice. And, of course, an endless supply of small work may make you long for meatier projects with bigger clients.

Ultimately, which you choose should be right for you as an individual and right for your business. As with anything I've said in this book, it shouldn't be based on what someone else does or says, and you're probably bored of me saying that by now. Miracles can happen on any size wave, a surfing analogy that I love, meaning you are rewarded for getting up on your board regardless of the size of the wave you surf. The key is to pay attention to the individual client and not their size, as we should be striving to build genuine connections, and this means inherently not viewing prospects as just a ticket item, regardless of its size.

### Managing emotions

Providing creativity for sale can be a rollercoaster of emotions. When your work is on show for everyone to see, everyone can judge it. The very nature of making creative work for public consumption means that people can easily make up their mind about how skilful, creative, and talented you are, all without ever talking to you directly, and this can be hard to take. When your brand of creativity is also your identity, it can be hard to keep a lid on your emotions when things get tough, and people are critical.

This is one thing when it's a stranger on the internet hating on your designs, but what about when it's a client? If a client doesn't like a piece of work but you truly believe it's what's best for the brand, then you, like most creatives, will want to fight your corner and defend your work. But while less-than-positive feedback can feel like a dagger to the heart, don't let your pride be the reason you're fighting. The essence of creativity means we are all coming at it from a subjective perspective, and you should try to squish your damaged ego back down and instead ask yourself:

— Can the work in question be improved, and if so, how?
— What should be left alone?
— How can I give and take feedback more constructively?

When you've set aside your ego, emotions, and subjectivity, you might realise that the client is right. In this case, think about the people who will ultimately be encountering and using the thing you're making or creating. Or if you still really believe in your creation and its end-user-applicability, then you can fight for it — and the better your communication skills, the better you can make a case for why it works or why it doesn't. What's crucial is putting the end user front and centre, so your ego can step aside on this one.

## Keeping your eyes open

With any project, it's important to take the time to observe it as a whole. Of course, you should fulfil your role and stay in your lane, but you should also take note of what other people are doing to make sure you're being your best self. For a solo freelancer, this might mean keeping an eye on what other team members or talents in the process are doing, if such information is available, and how the various cogs in the process fit together. For a project manager of a small creative business, this means staying in the loop with what your team is doing, even if you're not personally delivering the work. Either way, you should be paying attention to what goes well and what goes badly.

Crucially, understanding every working part of a project, big or small, means you're well-placed to cover anything that might go wrong, whether it's within your own team or something missing from the client's process. You'll be able to see things that others might miss and identify things that could be improved.

This broader curiosity will help you grow, and it might even help you help the client further. Let's say you're designing a website for a client and noticed they're lacking GDPR-compliant cookies and data handling policies, so you mention it to the client and offer to help them out with this work if they need it. The result is a win-win; the client avoids potentially costly legal problems, and you land some extra work and keep the client extra happy.

Of course, this doesn't mean you should be intrusive; it just means you should keep your eyes open and make sure you're learning from the experience and wisdom of the people around you. Having a long-term vision for your creative business should go hand in hand with a desire to learn and improve. When you eventually lead on projects, you will be a lot more confident in running a tight operation if you've been studying how projects actually work. When you start considering even the smallest parts of the project, even when you don't have to, you start the next chapter of your career.

## Dealing with enquiries

Turning an enquiry into an actual project can feel like a project of its own, but it doesn't have to. Generally, it's inexperience that leads to wasted time here, and in the early days, I was caught out by weeks of back-and-forth emails with potential clients that led nowhere and submitted numerous idea proposals for projects where it turned out the client didn't want to pay.

Downloadable templates for email scripts can be accessed via the bonus content.

**Avoiding a tennis match** - The first thing you have to understand is that enquiries are usually written, mostly through email, or sometimes through DMs on social media. A few people still use the telephone for enquiries, but it's a smaller percentage these days than back in the day. These initial messages are often very basic and incomplete, and the problem with this is that it becomes very easy to get lost in long exchanges. The more detail you go into in your emails, the more time you lose. You know your offer, you know your prices, and you want to know more about the project, so don't get pulled into an email tennis match that might not produce a winner. It's in our nature to want to make people happy and provide solutions, but even as a small operation, your time is precious.

To solve this, set up an automated email template that shows your interest in discussing the project further. Remember the five-sentence rule. Ask the prospect to get on a phone or video call and to share their project brief in the meantime if they haven't already. You can even set up a booking system such as Calendly, offering 15-30-minute time slots to discuss their enquiry. This will save you endless hours that could be used elsewhere to grow your business.

**Dealing with holiday enquiries -** Ask anyone in the creative industry about the number of 'dream' projects that land in their inbox just as they are on the way to the airport for their well-earned holiday. It might be our version of the full moon, but it happens so often it must be more than just an industry myth. To make it even more humorous, I've seen people tweeting about packing for holiday to tempt their destiny for the work to land in their inbox. It's a silly joke but it happens.

The traditional way to deal with your enquiries in your absence is to set up an 'out of office' message to tell people you're sunning it up somewhere. If your prospect is in a hurry to decide who to commission, this might kill off the line of enquiry right away, even if the work won't be starting for a while after you're back. Some people like to be hasty; others don't have a choice.

Instead, you could set up an automated email system asking for more questions about the brief and proposing a call for when you're back. That way, you can enjoy a glass of champagne at the airport knowing you're not killing off a possible opportunity in your absence. If the prospect is serious, they'll be booking a call while you're working out how much 100ml of combined liquids is to pass security, that fun pre-holiday quiz we could all do without.

**Meeting the prospective client** - In my opinion, it's paramount to speak to a prospective client on the phone or video call before committing, rather than just a chain of emails. This is because you can quickly and easily determine whether the project fits your criteria and meets your values, and a lot more. While the conversation should, for the most part, focus on the project itself – the client's ambition, strategy, plan (if they have one), hopes, and fears, you should also discuss the project's value.

A call can confirm whether you like the client (and vice versa) and whether your communication and working styles are compatible. You don't want to be stuck on a year-long project with someone you struggle to work with as neither of you will get the best from one another. That way, you can keep your operations running, keep your client happy, and keep your sanity intact.

**Things to check on the call with a client:**
— What do they want? Does it make sense?
— Is this the type of work you normally do?
— Are they asking you to do what you don't do?
— Does the work align with your values?
— How did they get here and why are they looking for someone new? What other creatives are being considered for this project, if they're willing to tell you?
— Who is making the decision on how to proceed?
— What was their reason to get in touch with you specifically?

**Warning signs to look out for with prospective clients:**
— Trying hard to haggle a discount
— In a hurry and not listening to realistic timelines
— Client values don't align with yours
— Speaks about their ego instead of the work
— Not paying attention to the process breakdown
— Keeps talking about the price
— Fishing for a cost without commitment
— Promising a lot of future work but wants to start with a bargain

**And a few tips that may or may not seem obvious:**
— Never ask a prospect what they think the solution is to their problem. Always make them talk about the problem first and any implications of it not being solved
— Make the client feel listened to by letting them speak and repeating key points back to them. Take your time to really, really listen and find clues to identify the issues.

— Don't expect to solve the whole problem in one call or meeting. Never commit to timelines during the meeting; take time to plan and at a more appropriate time

It can be easy to point out what we think the problem is before we've heard about and understood the situation in its entirety, and it's not uncommon for a logo designer to confidently shoot down an existing identity, with the confidence of a penalty taker, only for them to find out they are aiming at their own goal. Don't be so hasty. If you jump straight in pointing out bad logos, dicey office design, flimsy copy, or bad UX, you might be right, but you've not yet had time to prove yourself or even listen to a client's concerns, so hold back.

**Deciding whether to submit a proposal -** As we talked about in the last chapter, it's all too easy to be seduced into taking on a project with a scope that's bigger than you can handle and biting off more than you can chew. By all means, if you see an opportunity to turn a small project into a bigger chunk of work, then go for it. A creative challenge like this is often the perfect setup to learn and grow your skill stack. Stepping out of your lane can sometimes be a route worth making; it might keep things moving and take you in unprecedented directions that can yield new opportunities.

But, from my personal experience, it can also be a risky bet. While you might feel an initial elation when you land a bigger job, you'll likely be feeling the opposite if you struggle to land a tricky and nuanced brief that seemed straightforward in your head. Often, our creative minds can lead us to believe we're an invincible problem-solver only to look foolish when the results are not quite as we promised. The trick is to take on reasonable size challenges, ones that push you somewhat out of your comfort zone but not the whole way out. Contrary to what some people say, the magic doesn't happen when you're entirely out of the comfort zone but when you have one shoe in and one out. And you should always have a plan to get yourself out if you fall down a hole.

If you get an enquiry that's outside your normal scope, bear this balancing act in mind. Sometimes, sticking to your niche can pay dividends. Other times, what you offer isn't in demand and you might need to re-evaluate what you offer, especially if your incoming enquiries are for something you don't offer but potentially could. Let's say you want to make film posters but keep getting enquiries to design websites in the film industry — could you expand your offering? While I'm not saying overhaul everything you've built, I am saying that it often pays to be flexible and follow the flow of the work, growing both your bank balance and your skill stack.

**Quoting confidently -** If you decide to submit a proposal, then you need to learn the art of quoting confidently. I learned this lesson, once again, from a builder.

Back in the day, I needed someone to fix a few things in my house. Handyman companies are not exactly known for their brilliant branding; after all, they're in the business of fixing domestic infrastructure problems, not their kerning skills, and this business was no different. So, after the work was done, I was chatting to the business owner and told him what I do for a living and how I could improve their branding and identity to make their company look more trustworthy and established. The business owner was genuinely interested, and we discussed the possible deliverables, then he asked me for a quote. But despite the chat, I didn't end up submitting a quote as I assumed I was wasting my time and that the company couldn't afford my services.

Months later, I needed some work done so I called the same company. The bill for the work ended up being the exact same price I was going to quote them for my work. I immediately felt foolish for not sending them a quote. The company, as it turned out, had more than enough cash to afford the work. Ever since then, I've made sure I don't hesitate; if the moment is right, I explain what I do and what it costs, then let them make the decision for themselves.

**Taking rejection** - It's human nature to feel annoyed and deflated if an inquiry promises the earth but never becomes a reality. But you should never get too excited about the prospect of what might be until all is said and done, and the invoice is paid too. Until then, it's speculative and uncertain.

And just like everything in life, not everything will work out and some things are not meant to be.

Again, you need to separate your emotions from the business, accepting that your creative offer isn't for everyone, and you are not the right person for everyone.

**Cutting the cord** - Likewise, sometimes you need to be the one who pulls the plug. You can't force chemistry, and some people are just not meant to work together. It might seem crazy to kill off a project that could have been very lucrative, but ultimately, it's not worth it in some cases. Trust your gut rather than going into something that feels wrong just for the money. This way, you will end up with the right commissions and projects to suit what you do.

## Doing the work

Congrats! You got the work. It might feel like the pitching or negotiation process was hard work, but now the real work begins. The following pointers will make the process of actually doing the work as smooth and satisfying as possible — and keep the extra admin to a minimum.

**Being ambitious but realistic -** Not every client will want to reinvent the wheel right away, but a great collaboration starts when you're both looking to the future and feel that anything could be possible. Being ambitious while remaining realistic brings an energy to the project that can drive progress. Being realistic means starting the project with a clear brief and defined deliverables. Always outline your process to show how you can deliver what's agreed.

**Getting un-stuck -** We all get stuck from time to time, but 'creative block' is often rooted in far less lofty and more practical shortcomings than we might expect. It can be down to an overwhelming number of available options that need filtering down to one idea. It can be bad planning, or no understanding of what we need to do due to a poor brief from the client. It can be a lack of collaborators to help you with the project. It can be a fear of actually getting started. As you become experienced, you'll find that these blockages occur far less frequently, but in the meantime, if you find yourself blocked, take a break and ask yourself what the actual problem is. Talk it through with someone else to the solution. If you want more tips on this topic, check out my other book *Mindful Creative*.

**Avoiding the awkward preview -** A new client often wants to see 'something' fairly quickly. You have your methods, processes, and timings, yet sometimes you might get asked if you can share previews early. Naturally, that probably means sending work that isn't ready for other eyes. The result? The client sees the preview and prematurely worries about your ability to do the job well — even if you warned them that the work wasn't ready and they didn't listen. In these situations, it's important to politely push back, stand your ground, and maintain your integrity to your craft. This alone should prove your dedication to, and ability within, your craft. And to avoid being asked for early previews, always negotiate a realistic timeline that gives you enough time to do your best work away from impatient, prying eyes.

**Knowing your limits** - Even the most experienced multidisciplinary creative will burn out if they have to do the work of an entire team. It might feel rewarding to deliver every part of the work (and clients often want to cut corners by scrimping on budget and not hiring as many people as they should), but the hours and effort will see you run out of steam, too exhausted to even think about the project anymore. So, make sure you have the right resources in place for the job at hand.

**Keeping the client in the loop -** There's one or two, or twenty-two, clues in this book that I don't like long emails. I see emails as a doorbell, a signal that someone is there, not a place to spend hours on nuanced notes that only end up being misunderstood or staying unread. Instead, before you send a piece of work to the client, record a video of yourself with a quick narration of what's been done, how it works, and what is still outstanding, then include any questions you need answers to (Loom is great software for this). Doing so will save you endless hours and speed up your workflow, though keep a written note of any important points so they're easily found when searching later.

Also bear in mind that everyone is different, and you might find that your client doesn't like videos or would prefer to communicate via email for the most part. Ideally, you should discuss your communication preferences and strive to find a harmonious balance that works for both of you.

**Moving the goalposts -** Even a well-defined project can deviate from the original brief or balloon in size. If the client keeps asking for extra deliverables resulting in extra hours, you might feel obliged to do the extra work, and you might feel it will make your project look more accomplished. But this can easily slip into spending every waking hour working on a project that doesn't pay anymore.

My own horror story is a 4-hour phone call for a logo project that earned me next to nothing. Keep an eye on the scope and be vocal about it if things creep (which is why a lot of creative contracts have a clause for 'scope creep') unless the client has long-term value and is worth going the extra, extra mile for. Clients can become friends, and they can also become exceptional time thieves.

**Being reliable every time -** No matter how good you are, how great your ideas might be, or how well you can use your creative software, if you don't deliver the right stuff on time and every time, that client probably won't bother contacting you again. As I said before, reliability is the key to long-term success.

Clients like freelancers who are keen, but this can mean nothing if they don't stick to their timelines and deadlines. If the timelines are slipping, speak up. Be honest with the client about where you're at with the work, admit any issues you're facing, and explain why the original timescales are delayed. People will understand if, and only if, you're up-front and honest.

I get it; long projects can become miserable, and you can sometimes spend what feels like a lifetime working on some projects, wading through treacle. When you're stuck in the middle of it with no end in sight, it's easy to let it consume you. But if it gets too much, speak up. Be honest and upfront — and ask for some extra time to give you some breathing space.

**Delivering the right goods** - This might sound obvious but double-check the project brief before submitting the work to ensure that everything is being delivered in the correct format and size, and in the right place.

If you provide a download link for the client, test the link first and make sure the work is correctly labelled and organised in the right folders.

Creative projects can take a lot out of you, even the ones that go really well, but don't take your eye off the ball at the last moment before delivery.

**Asking for feedback -** When everything goes well, it's the stuff dreams are made of. When you fall short, it's often tempting to write off a project due to reasons you consider to be outside your control. Instead, you should ask the client for performance feedback regardless of the outcome. Always find out how your business is working from the point of view of your clients, as they might just know you better than you know yourself and give you helpful pointers to get better or even better.

**Putting your soul into what you do -** Anyone who cares about their work will feel a sense of attachment to the results, but great work doesn't happen by accident; it's a process that should be nurtured from start to finish. By contrast, if you rush your work, people will see through it. If you bullshit your ideas, people will see through it. If you cut corners or don't understand the scope, people will see through it. If you're in it for the money, people will see through it. But if you do your work for the right reasons, put your soul into what you do, and make your creativity the thing you stand for, then people will appreciate it and stick around for more.

All of your efforts in building your brand of creativity and business are made worthwhile with every project that you deliver well. The circle is completed.

Creativity for Sale

Pages

# 192–205

Section - no.8
# Tools

Creativity for Sale

Chapter - no.8

**197.** Business tools
**198.** Accounting
**198.** *Time management*
**198.** Client management
**198.** *Personal management*
**198.** Social media
**200.** *Automation tools*
**200.** Creative tools
**202.** *People tools*
**202.** The future is creative

Creativity for Sale

## Tools

You've won the client, and you're making money. Rinse and repeat. Surely, it's that simple right? Well, in some ways, it can be that simple and in other ways, it's most certainly not. When you've only got one or two clients, and it's just you doing the work, then it can be relatively easy to manage everything. But as soon as your operation starts increasing in size or complexity, then it really helps if you have tools to keep things running smoothly. And it's far easier to put those tools in place when your business is simple than when you're on the backfoot further down the line.

### Business tools

Bad news first: creative people are often pretty bad at running their operation using tools and time-saving products. Good news next: those who do get good at this find their business life much easier. There are plenty of apps and tools to help you run your business and make you look like a professional from day one. Yes, you'll need to spend a bit of time playing around with these tools, especially if you're not tech-savvy, but it's worth it because they will save a lot more time later — time you can spend on being creative.

## Accounting

Most creatives find the finance and accounting side of things a yawn-fest. Some creatives can't even get their head around balance sheets and the like, let alone figure out their yearly tax return. That's why it's worth using a bookkeeping and accounting tool to keep your accounts in check. There are free and paid versions of accounting software, and which you choose really depends on your needs, but all of them take a lot of the headache out of accounting. If you still don't feel keen or confident, getting an actual accountant is a must.

**Tools** — Freeagent, Xero, Quickbooks, Sage

## Time management

Many creatives also find project management a challenge, and our creative, exciting way of working doesn't run smoothly with being organised and methodical. That's why time, task, and project management apps are an absolute necessity for creatives, especially as your client base and team grows. Again, some of these tools are free while others are paid-for, and many have both free and paid versions depending on the complexity of your requirements. You might start out with a free tool, then eventually pay for something more bespoke when you need it.

**Tools** — Asana, Slack, Monday, Hive, Trello, Miro

## Client management

As well as managing the project itself, there are aspects of working with clients that are easily solved by tech, such as document signing programs to ensure the client has signed the contract, calendar apps to schedule meetings and calls, pipeline tracking tools to keep an eye on your leads, and screen capture software so you can record videos for your clients.

**Tools** — DocuSign, Adobe Sign, Calendly, Google Meet, Zoom, Pipe Drive, HubSpot, Loom, Frame.io

## Personal management

The wonder of tech isn't just in what it can do for your business but what it can do for you personally. There are apps to store your notes and harness your creativity, apps to block social media to help you focus, and apps to track your time so you know how long things take and how productive you are.

**Tools** — Notion, Evernote + many more

## Social media

While social media can feel like a nightmare, there are many tools that will help you run it without losing your time and your mind. Some enable you to schedule posts in advance, track your analytics better, or even plan digital campaigns.

**Tools** — Later.com, ContentCal, Meta Business Suite, Hootsuite

## Automation tools

And finally, once your tech setup is expanding, there are tools that help you with other tools, such as automating certain actions and connecting various technologies together so you can eliminate a lot of unnecessary admin tasks.

**Tools** — Zapier, IFTTT, Make

Now you've got your brand-new, shiny business tools, you might find it a bit overwhelming trying to use them all in your business. I totally understand this, but bear in mind that tools are just instruments, and they're here to make your life more harmonious. Many of these tools are here to solve the problem of time vs. admin, not to make your life more difficult. So, if you find that a tool isn't helpful, then scrap it and try something else. There's plenty out there for everyone.

## Creative tools

As a creative professional, there are many tools and software programs that will make your creative life easier and many that are simply a necessity to do the work your clients require. Which of these you need really depends on the specific type of work you do. And indeed, these are not the only tools available, nor the ones that might stay popular or even stay around forever, but there will always be more tools available for these tasks, so pick the ones that work for you.

**Photography & Design** — Adobe Creative Cloud, Gimp, Canva, Affinity, Kritta, ProCreate, Inkspace
**3D apps** — Blender, Spline, Cinema 4D, Redshift, Houdini
**Web & UI design** — Sketch, Figma, Adobe XD, Invision
**Website builders** — SquareSpace, Wix, WordPress, Editor X, Framer, Webflow, Bootstrap
**Online stores** — Shopify, WooCommerce, Big Cartel, SquareSpace, Magento, Weebly
**SEO and PPC** — Semrush, Botify, The Hoth
**Email marketing** — Mailchimp, Klaviyo, ConverterKit, Author.Email, MailerLite, Flow, Buffer
**Podcast production** — Riverside FM, Simplecast, Acast, Squadcast, Zencaster
**Music and audio production** — Adobe Audition, Ableton, Soundcloud, Audacity

Ultimately, creative tools are here to help you improve at your craft and deliver a better outcome to your clients. While the learning curve might sometimes be steep, they should help you do a better job. As a professional, you should be on an endless quest to learn more and improve, whether it's new creative software or a new technique. And if you're stuck with a technical issue, it goes without saying that YouTube tutorials are a good place to start.

## People tools

Did I just call people 'tools'? Erm, yes, I did. What I mean by that is: other people are often very good ways to learn and improve yourself. While it's not as simple as just downloading some software or installing an app, you should always surround yourself with wiser people, whether it's joining a community of fellow creatives or getting yourself a business mentor. If that's not possible, consider courses or coaching programmes to give you a view into other worlds.

**Tools** — Meetup groups, Networking events, Mentors, Coaches, Accountability buddies, Training courses, Coaching programmes, Podcasts, TED talks

You get the picture, right? Sometimes, these tools will cost money and other times, hours. Either way, investment in your progress will always be money well-spent.

## The future is creative

It's unarguable that an increasing number of tasks have been, and will continue to be, automated, whether through software or machinery. Since Johannes Gutenberg invented the printing press in 1450 (and likely long before that), new technologies that transform creative work have terrified people. Today, such technologies are emerging faster than at any other time in history, and there are endless people talking about AI and what it might mean for jobs, be it creative jobs or otherwise. However, it's worth looking back and recalling how every new tool has been accompanied by fears that it will 'kill off' its less-advanced predecessor. Bear in mind that social media didn't replace IRL socialising, Kindle e-books didn't replace printed books, and streaming didn't sound the death knell for vinyl records.

AI won't take all of our jobs, nor make us inherently less creative. Indeed, I would argue that creativity is the only thing that cannot truly be automated, even using the most advanced generative rolls or machine learning programmes. Pure, true creativity needs context, journey, and a meaningful outcome to make people experience something. Creativity is defined as *"the use of skill and imagination to produce something new or to produce art"* [Oxford Learner's Dictionary, 2023], and by this definition, AI inherently cannot be creative as it must rely on information and ideas that already exist in order to generate new ones. However smart its prompts or capabilities are, it can never think like a person for a person.

And so, creativity will always be a skill that's in demand. After all, someone has to create these tools. People are always the drivers, and they are the ones who make the tools for other people. AI can certainly be a supremely powerful tool in its generative capacity and power to streamline and speed up various processes, but the ability to finesse a piece of work that connects with another person's imagination and inspires emotion is a very human one.

On the contrary, rather than fearing new technological advancements, we should consider it a privilege to live and work at a time where such tools exist, as they can help us on our own journey. What's more, there's literally no point panicking about emerging technologies as more will always come. Instead, we should learn to enjoy and appreciate the chance to be part of the future, focusing on what we can control rather than what we can't control. So, don't fear new tech and tools — remember, you're creating with people and for people.

"For the best return on your money, pour your purse into your head."

Benjamin Franklin

Creativity for Sale

Pages

# 206–227

Chapter - no.9
# Grow

Creativity for Sale

## Chapter - no.9

**211.** Grow forever
**212.** *Spinning plates*
**214.** Marginal gains
**215.** *Track your progress*
**217.** Grow from your mistakes
**218.** *Grow your team*
**220.** Consider cognitive diversity
**222.** *Choosing your problems*
**223.** Grow your reputation
**224.** *Growing through change*

Creativity for Sale

## Grow

You've reached the final chapter of this book, which means you're almost ready to set sail on your own voyage. But before you go, I want you to grow. Wait, what did I just say? Yes, this chapter is all about your growth as a creative professional, because if I haven't made it abundantly clear enough on our journey together so far, succeeding in the long term with your creative business requires you to personally keep growing. So, grab a pot and some soil, and let's get planting.

### Grow forever

Running your own creative business is the ultimate opportunity to make each day more exciting than the last. Your creative business is constantly moving forward, and once your project has been delivered, it's on to the next, and the next, and the next. Embrace the fact that what you've created so far, for others or for yourself, will need to be improved, tweaked, or adapted as a result of new findings, feedback, or changes in market conditions.

It would be easy to think you're doing it all once and forever, but the truth is that you're doing it once now and you'll do it again and again in the future. The quicker you embrace this fact, the easier your business life will be. If you don't accept this fact, you will either fight against change, which is exhausting, or you will find yourself left in the doldrums as the world moves on.

## Spinning plates

When you become more successful and land more and more clients, you inevitably end up spinning a lot of plates. Some of these plates are the day-to-day operations that keep the business running, and it can feel like they're in direct conflict with the creative stuff or sap energy that you could be putting into actual client work, which ironically are often the other plates you need to keep spinning to pay the bills. Despite it being 'what you do', these creative commissions can easily drain your time, and before you know it, you're working every waking hour for everyone but yourself.

I get this, believe me, but even if time and energy are in short supply, you need to keep reserves dedicated to the tasks and ideas that are solely related to your business, not just doing the work and doing the admin. This means taking time to keep in touch with previous clients, get in touch with new prospects, pay compliments to other brands, revise the copy on your website, post snaps on your business social media, comment on industry thought pieces, and scope out potential collaborators.

While these might not seem essential, they are the future lifeblood of your business. If you run out of work, have projects put on hold, or have clients cancel, what would your business look like if you hadn't been doing these 'unessential' tasks? Of course, a break can be a healthy refresher that enables you to take some time to reflect on where you are professionally on your journey, but it's not easy to reflect if you're worrying about paying the bills, and most business owners don't get to take a break when the work runs out. The reality is, if you have no leads in the pipeline, you'll probably end up trying to find more work in a desperate panic, and that rarely leads to good choices.

As well as the business and marketing activities, you also need to carve out time for your personal development, such as learning new skills or applications, a bit like staying in good shape physically. Every skill is a muscle that needs working out to stay in its best condition.

While spinning a bunch of plates can seem like an exhausting prospect, dropping them takes even more energy as you have to pick them up and attempt to glue the pieces back together. So, ultimately, you should be striving to improve your capacity to spin plates. Sometimes, this means passing plates onto others who are capable; other times, it means being more discerning about which plates you accept; and other times, it means being more organised in your planning to spin the plates without any of them falling.

## Marginal gains

Sir Dave Brailsford, former performance director of British Cycling, revolutionised the sport by using his theory of 'marginal gains'.

The idea is that if you break absolutely everything down into its component parts, then improve every tiny part by 1%, you will get a significant improvement when you put it all back together. In other words, the cumulative benefits can be extraordinary. The concept can also allow you to improve your overall performance in work and life, undestanding that small incremental gains over time add up to big outcomes.

The concept of marginal gains in the world of creativity and small business can be applied in a simple yet effective way. Just as a road cyclist, you can apply the concept to your operations and make tiny, frequent improvements across your whole range of ideas and activities as a business owner.

Here are some actions to kickstart the chain reaction to cumulative benefits:
— Improve your messaging
— Improve your branding and update your stationery
— Analyse your website traffic and improve your keywords
— Improve your pipeline and reach out to existing clients
— Begin a personal project as a conversation starter with new audiences
— Outsource your admin tasks to earmark time for your creative gains

— Review your performance feedback
— Speed up your workflow with automation tools
— Get a mentor
— Search for courses that add to your skill stack
— Get up to speed on the latest technology developments
— Look outside your industry for inspiration and information
— Read a book on topics related to your work
— Watch a TED talk, watch a Masterclass, or listen to a podcast

It might not be possible to attend to each of these ideas in an orderly fashion, and sometimes you have to troubleshoot as you see things that need improvement. However, marginal gains are not an excuse to procrastinate instead of tackling your current projects. If I'm faced with something complicated that needs my full attention, I tend to divert to something simpler like changing my email signature or planning my next website. It's more of an excuse instead of a strategic decision. On the contrary, these small improvements should be part of the workflow alongside the main schedule, not in place of it.

## Track your progress

If we ever meet in the future, prepare yourself that I am going to ask you how it's all going. Whether it's in person or digitally, if we exchange a few words, I will be curious to see how my suggestions have worked out for you. And when you get asked how it's all going, only you'll know the answer to that. How well you can answer depends on whether you've been actively tracking your progress or not.

In the early days, I made the mistake of not tracking my progress, beyond the knowledge that financially, I'll survive for another month or year. But to keep improving, I realised I needed to be aware of the progress I was making. This is very difficult to do if we have no idea how we're doing. It's tempting to think that we'll remember the highlights and the lessons, but in the day to day of spinning the plates, we inevitably lose track — and when making 1% marginal gains, it can be difficult to see our small but significant improvements over time.

If we don't see the results we want when we want, we can be guilty of thinking that our efforts are futile. This is a reminder that it takes time for things to take off, and progress is a long-term thing. This doesn't mean waste time thinking where you want to be in five years' time as you might be in a totally different position and have a totally different mindset as a result of your actions today. It means planting your seeds and letting them grow — allowing time for disappointment, elation, heartache, progress, strife, and a plethora of other feelings.

When you're running your own business, you won't have someone behind you to fall back on or push you to keep growing. The level of self-motivation required to keep progressing can become draining, but it's important to keep digging deep every time. Keep setting personal benchmarks and nudge them a bit higher every so often.

Knowing that you're pushing to be the best version of yourself should motivate you, even when times get tough.

## Grow from your mistakes

When you last messed up, how did you feel? Did you have that gut-wrenching feeling that you're the only person who could have made that mistake? How could you make such a rookie, sloppy mistake when the world around you is getting everything right? Everyone feels like this from time to time, but you'll shed this feeling as soon as you accept that everyone has done something similar at some point. We're all human, and we all make silly mistakes at times.

You can't eliminate mistakes and you'll make a fair few throughout your career, so when you inevitably do, you should strive to learn from them. Every time you are accountable for your failures, you will own them and learn. Each time you succeed in not repeating a past mistake, you will grow. And reverse-engineering this, it means to grow, you have to make mistakes. Mistakes are the fastest way of teaching us what works and what doesn't.

For nearly a decade, I've been lucky to live in a house that overlooks a golf course. The expansive gorgeous green space is often populated by strolling figures with golf irons. It's not a place for the likes of Tiger Woods though, just a local course on the edge of the city. But the spectacle I get to see is often more entertaining than high-paying sports TV broadcasts.

I quickly learned that a golfer who isn't very good is called 'a hacker', and there's no short supply of them. They get excellently worked up when they fluff their shot. They hit their ball, the turf is flying high, yet the ball is leisurely on its way to nowhere.

The hacker gets angry as if they just lost a bet with Tiger Woods to the tune of a few million dollars. It's always fascinating seeing their raw belief at the shot in reality vs. what they were imagining.

We are all 'hackers' in our own way. We pre-empt the shots we take: a client project, a presentation, a new skill. And when we fluff the shot, we smash our iron on the turf angrily. We blame the iron, the grass, the weather, a squirrel in the distance distracting us. We don't attribute the mistake to our aim, our lack of focus, or our lack of practice, and let's be honest, it's often easier to blame things outside our control.

It's also easy to turn our anger on ourselves and say, "I'm just useless" or "I'm shit at golf!" It's easy to shove the irons to the back of the cupboard and hang up our golfing gloves. And while we might not see this as blaming things outside our control, it is really, because we're not taking accountability for why we fluffed the shot and what we can do to get better next time.

It's not surprising really, because the internet has glorified excellence and made everyone look like superhumans who make the shot first time, every time. The reality is, getting better at most things is within our control — if we put in the time and effort. So, try again, and take better aim over and over again until you can do it with your eyes closed.

## Grow your team

Whether it's your determination, resilience, or drive to deliver, your superpower can give you a competitive advantage over your peers. It can work like 12 cups of coffee, encouraging you to stay up and work endless hours to get a project over the line. And while this will keep your clients happy and bring you success for a while, there will come a time when you're exhausted from doing long days and late nights.

The problem is, a bit like with your motivation, there is often no one to fall back on, especially in the early days when it's just you keeping your business going. And you can justify this solo work for a while, telling yourself it's more lucrative to deliver a complex piece of work without needing to pay anyone else (which is true), and that clients like having one person to deal with for the whole project (which is true). But it's also true that going it alone can mean sacrificing the most valuable commodity of all: time.

Ask yourself whether you're really working alone because your budget won't stretch to bringing in help or whether you're afraid of ceding control. Or the plethora of other reasons you might be avoiding expanding your business beyond yourself, which might be perfectionism, a fear of failure, or even a fear of success.

Now ask yourself what will happen if you keep working flat out on your own. The answer to this, even if you don't want to admit it, is that your tiredness will cause you to make more mistakes and you'll be too tired to learn from them. Or you will eventually get burnt out and maybe even want to hang up your business hat with your golf gloves. Or you'll stick at it but ironically become the blocker that stops your business from growing and progressing.

To claw back some time for yourself, you have to loosen your grip and let others get involved. And while you might imagine losing all control, it can actually do wonders for opening up new ideas, styles, and approaches that you hadn't thought of or don't have the skills to do. So, see the help as an investment in your freedom, rather than as a threat to your ego or a hit to your bank balance.

Start weighing up the value of time vs. money (vs. everything else that might be holding you back from having a team). Is keeping all of the income really worth sacrificing your time (and eventually, probably your health)? Is protecting your ego and clinging onto control worth the stress of having to do everything yourself?

It can take a lifetime to strike the right balance, but if you're bogged down with endless deadlines and an impossible workload, you leave no space for the imaginative leaps that time provides the space for. Your creativity, and life in general, are all the richer for some time out.

And to go back to the issue of pricing from earlier in the book, you will need to reconsider your pricing to account for bringing someone else in. On a small scale, at the start, this may mean outsourcing parts of the work to other freelancers, ensuring that you cover the cost of paying them and make a profit yourself. On a big scale, when you can afford to, this may mean hiring your own employees.

## Consider cognitive diversity

If (and hopefully when) you start to build a team, one thing to bear in mind is striving to ensure creative and cognitive diversity. This means having a team that offers a wealth of different life experiences, skill stacks, cultural backgrounds, personality traits, and opinions. This brings about a wonderful collision of new ideas and talents that simply can't be accessed when you're stuck in an echo chamber, talking to yourself or to people who are carbon copies of you.

While it's tempting to build a team of people who are just like you, the aim should be to expand your horizons. Just like the 'growth happens with one foot in and out of the comfort zone' idea from earlier, your business grows when you have a team of people who are similar in some ways but different in others. In that way, you can get along and work harmoniously while also challenging each other constructively and learning from your varied experience.

When people consider the notion of 'a meeting of minds and talents', the metaphor that often comes up is a vibrant, cosmopolitan metropolis where collaborators from across the globe are working in one place. Indeed, I've met plenty of creative teams working together in a city or country where none of them were born. Indeed, global diversity can often make for an even more successful project thanks to the range of different cultures and thought processes it brings.

But it's also the case that, today, we no longer need every collaborator to be in the same physical space, as we can grow multitalented multinational teams anywhere thanks to technology. In these remote teams, how we connect and collaborate is important to the creative process, not where we are in the world. Just make sure you factor in language barriers and time zones.

## Choosing your problems

A creative business is rarely all about creativity, and it often might not resemble a business too much either. A lot of the time, your role is to act as a therapist, life coach, cheerleader, or shoulder to cry on, whether it's for your team or your clients. You are the client's bridge between their aspirations and reality. As such, every new project is as much about the human aspects of dealing with people as it is about doing business and being creative.

Often, projects involve individuals or groups of people working together for the first time, whether it's you and a client, a client hiring a bunch of freelancers, or a creative business starting out with their own new team. On these occasions, everyone will generally come together to get the job done. Even if occasionally life gets in the way, it's often dealt with behind the scenes, with an air of professionalism and pragmatism. But occasionally, you will need to step in and solve the problem, and this requires three things: proactivity, confidence, and great communication skills.

If you see something going wrong, don't leave it until the plates stop spinning and hit the floor. If the problem is within your own team, then proactively and kindly speak to the relevant parties to see how you can solve the problem together. If they need to step back from the project, then you will have time to replace them thanks to your proactivity. If you see the problem occurring within the client's team setup, confidently and constructively raise it with them, with a solution to fix it.

Like mistakes, you can't avoid problems, and they will inevitably occur in business. As I said earlier, even blockbuster budgets don't guarantee zero issues. But you can often choose your problems wisely by proactively scoping out projects and clients before committing, choosing the right projects and clients for you, and choosing the right team for your business, which is everything we've been working towards up to this point.

You can also reduce the likelihood of problems occurring by proactively and confidently communicating early. If you set the project on the right course straight out of the harbour, then it's more likely to stay on course. This goes back to your first conversation with the client (remember that?), but it may also require regular reminders and steering. If you let your client or one of your team steer, and they've never been at the helm before, then you can quickly go off-course, lose momentum, or get stuck on the rocks. All metaphors aside, what this often translates to in real life is an endless stream of design feedback from the client.

Proactive, confident communication is the key to solving most problems, or preventing them from occurring in the first place.

## Grow your reputation

One bad review never killed a solid business, and likewise, one good review never stopped a bad business from failing. Your reputation is harvested over a long period of time, and it should be something you always keep in mind. As I've said many times (don't worry, I'm going to shut up soon), it's vital to be reliable and trustworthy, to deliver what you say you will (or more, in some cases), and to put your soul into what you do.

If you continue to do this, your reputation should grow organically, and you will find yourself getting recommended by former clients, getting repeat business, and developing a name for yourself. But as much as this 'word of mouth' approach is good, you should also keep a written track of your reputation, as this is also part of your progress. As I mentioned earlier, you should always ask your clients for feedback on your performance at the end of a project. Sometimes, this might be inward-facing feedback for your own learning and growth, but other times, this should be outward-facing feedback such as case studies, reviews, and testimonials to show other people what you can do.

And when you inevitably get one negative review or some less-than-stellar feedback, take the time to think about what went wrong and how you can put it right in the future.

## Growing through change

I promised I was going to shut up soon, and that time has almost arrived. But before I leave you to focus on your business, I have a final thought to leave you with.

You can put absolutely everything in place that we've discussed in this book, and you can feel like you're ready for the next level, but things don't always line up as you'd want them to. You might see your peers and competitors having breakthroughs, landing the clients you want, and getting their time in the industry spotlight, while you watch it all from afar.

It can be easy to believe you should be ahead on your journey, and even easier to buy into the mindset that you're already behind the curve. All of this can add up to anxiety and unhappiness. The truth is: every journey is unique and takes its own shape over time. You can spend a lifetime looking across the fence at how everybody else is doing but (other than occasional, construction market research), it will usually only make you feel worse. You are where you are right now, so find a way to enjoy it and keep growing. Things will change, and time will change, and eventually, you will see the fruits of your efforts.

In fact, change is the only thing for certain in life. Change is a sign of evolution and progress, and it's something we often say we yearn for but, in reality, fear. We are walking contradictions like that. We can't avoid change or stop it from happening, but we can take the time to understand what each change might entail and create, and how we can work with it and through it. Our personal and business circumstances are a small part of a much bigger picture that we ultimately can't control, but we can control how we react to change and what we make of it.

There's no crystal ball that can reveal the future of your creative career, and one day your role might be replaced by robots and your abilities might be superseded by AI. The world doesn't stand still, even if we do. However, being in the driving seat means you're in the right place to change lanes if you need to. This might mean a big shift like rebuilding your business, finding a new target audience, or developing a new skill. Either way, you may as well embrace change, as it's the only thing that's guaranteed, and find a way to use it for the good of your business.

And through every change, you have to keep driving. Contrary to what some career blogs will have you believe, the secret to a long-lasting successful business isn't talent, ideas, or skills. Obviously, these things are essential parts of running a creative business, but they are all for nothing if you, the one in the driving seat, don't show up day after day, week by week, month in and month out, year after year. The real trick in life is to keep showing up and keep moving forward — learning, growing, and improving through the challenges you face.

There will, inevitably, be tough times, but if you can retain your enthusiasm for your business, and live and breathe what you do, it's the sincerest form of creative marketing that exists. Genuine excitement about your work can't be faked; it comes from within, and people will queue up to work with you to get a taste of it.

Ultimately, this is what will keep you showing up, using your creativity for sale to put a smile on your clients' faces and bring their vision to life.

So, are you ready to catch another wave?

> "With the right mindset, we can't lose—we either practice what we've learned or we learn what we need to practice."

Noura

## Bonus Content

Visit **brandnubooks.co.uk** to access *Creativity for Sale* bonus content, including email scripts, list of tech tools, suggested reading list, image downloads, playlist links and more.

## Also available by Radim Malinic

**Book of Ideas** - Vol.1 - a journal of creative direction and graphic design / ISBN 978-0-9935400-0-4

**Book of Ideas** - Vol.2 - a journal of creative direction and graphic design / ISBN 978-0-9935400-1-1

**Book of Branding** - a guide to creating brand identity for startups and beyond / ISBN 978-0-9935400-3-5

**Pause, Breathe and Grow** - notes on mindful creative life ISBN 978-0-9935400-2-8

**Mindful Creative** - how to understand and deal with the highs and lows of creative life, career and business ISBN 978-0993540059 (also in audiobook)

**All titles are available in paperpack and kindle formats**

**brandnubooks.co.uk**

230

Creativity for Sale

229

Radim Malinic